Glory was in View

Glory Was in View
British Military Commanders of the American War of Independence 1775-83

W. H. Wilkin

LEONAUR

Glory Was in View
British Military Commanders of the American War of Independence 1775-83
by W. H. Wilkin

First published under the title
Some British Soldiers in America

Leonaur is an imprint of Oakpast Ltd

Copyright in this form © 2011 Oakpast Ltd

ISBN: 978-0-85706-749-4 (hardcover)
ISBN: 978-0-85706-750-0 (softcover)

http://www.leonaur.com

Publisher's Notes

Contents

Preface   7

Howe   11

Carleton   28

Clinton   43

Rawdon   62

Simcoe   74

Tarleton   93

Ferguson   114

Medows and Harris   130

Hale   160

Preface

The average Englishman knows very little of the war which raged from 1775 till 1783. If he thinks of it at all, he merely remembers Horace Walpole's remark about "*the war in which England saved a rock and lost a continent.*"

Even soldiers as a rule know hardly anything of the doings of their own regiments in North America during the Revolutionary War.

In 1862 Lord Wolseley (then a Colonel) entered Boston Harbour on his way to Montreal to take up a staff appointment in Canada. When an American gentleman pointed out Bunker's Hill, Colonel Wolseley remarked, "Ah! that was a dreadful disaster for us"; and in his autobiography he confesses the shame he felt when the American replied, "I beg your pardon, sir; Bunker's Hill was a victory for the English."

A little consideration will show that the British Army in North America would have no reason to shun comparison with its successors in South Africa, and the gallant deeds of the Boers in South Africa were certainly not surpassed by those of the Americans.

In 1775 the population of the United Kingdom was about 14,000,000, and the white population of the revolted colonies was between 2,000,000, and 3,000,000. The Royal Army in America (including Canada) never exceeded 50,000 men, yet it took the colonies more than seven years to secure their independence, and then they were only successful with the help of France.

In 1899 the population of the United Kingdom was about 40,000,000, while the Boer population of the two republics did not exceed 400,000. England had to maintain an army of 250,000 men in South Africa, and even then the war lasted more than two and a half years. During the century which intervened between the two wars, steam and electricity had done much to annihilate distance; improved means of communication had assisted co-operation between widely separated forces; and tinned foods rendered the task of maintaining an army in the field far less difficult. In both wars the enemy were far better supplied with information than the British troops. It is true that the invention of smokeless powder proved of great value to the Boers; but on the other hand the wooded nature of the country in which most of the fighting took place enabled the American colonists to conceal their numbers and dispositions.

In one respect the British Army was worse off in America than it was in South Africa. The colonists in America were men of British extraction, and thus the war was almost a civil war. Many officers, among them Sir William Howe, were very unwilling to serve against the Americans. General Amherst, the conqueror of Canada, actually declined the command of the army, and other officers remained on half-pay till the outbreak of war against France enabled them to serve their country against a foreign foe.

One cannot read about the American War of Independence without being struck by its similarity in many ways to the Anglo-Boer war in South Africa.

Americans are apt to resent the comparison, and to point out that they were successful whereas the Boers were not. They frequently ignore the fact that when they gained their independence, England was engaged in war against France, Spain, and Holland—the three strongest naval powers in Europe at that time; while Russia, Sweden, and Denmark formed the Armed Neutrality ready to join the Coalition should a favourable opportunity arise. Under similar circumstances no one would claim that we could have proved successful in South Africa. Moreover it is well to remember that the surrender of Yorktown, which practically decided the result of the war, was due to the French fleet obtaining the command of the sea for a time, and that 7,000 excellent French soldiers formed part of the attacking army, so that it is not without just cause that "Yorcktown" figures in the Gallery of Victories at Versailles.

It is a matter of common knowledge that the advice of Sir William Butler, the commander-in-chief in South Africa before the war, was disregarded.

In like manner Gage, the commander-in-chief in America, wrote as follows on October 30, 1774:

"If force is to be used at length, it must be a considerable one;

for to begin with small numbers will only encourage resistance and not terrify.

A little later he asked for 20,000 men, but his request was disregarded by the Ministry.

Lord Wolseley stated in the House of Lords that the advice which he gave at the time of the crisis in 1899 was ignored. In 1775 there was no commander-in-chief, but the adjutant-general, General Harvey, wrote on June 30 to Howe:

> Unless a settled plan of operations be agreed upon for next spring, our army will be destroyed by damned driblets.

The military authorities at home fully realized the gravity of the position, for on the same date General Harvey wrote:

> Taking America as it at present stands, it is impossible to conquer it with our British Army. To attempt to conquer it internally by our force is as wild an idea as ever controverted common sense.

It is well to remark that when these words were written England was not at war with any European power.

British officers who had served in North America did not underestimate the difficulties before them in the light-hearted manner of the politicians at home.

In both wars sound military plans were on various occasions subordinated to political considerations, with very serious results.

In South Africa the Boers wasted their strength before Mafeking and Kimberley, and the outbreak of the war found a small British force dangerously exposed at Dundee. In America the British operations, particularly in the south, were largely based on expected support from loyalists. The two greatest disasters which befell the Americans were both largely due to political causes. Fort Washington was only held out of deference to Congress, who had passed resolutions to that effect; and when Lincoln was considering the advisability of evacuating Charleston, the inhabitants insisted on the place being defended.

The eighteenth century is often regarded as a dull period, but the middle of that century marks a very interesting development in the history of the British Army. It was during the Seven Years' War that Stringer Lawrence and Clive—following the example set by the French—first showed what British officers could do with native troops. At the same time British and Colonial troops were fighting side by side against the French in America.

In the American War of Independence, British officers first showed their aptitude for commanding colonial irregulars, and in Tarleton's Legion and Simcoe's Rangers we see the predecessors of the Imperial Light Horse and other famous corps in South Africa.

It was inevitable from the nature of the fighting that in each war there should be a certain number of cases where the white flag was abused, and where irregulars, after offering to surrender, fired on the British troops; but it is truly lamentable that during the South African War, as in the eighteenth century, there existed Members of Parliament who were not ashamed to cheer when the news of British reverses was announced in the House of Commons.

The first three chapters deal with Howe, Carleton, and Clinton—the three commanders-in-chief. The fourth chapter deals with Rawdon, who gained the victory of Hobkirk's Hill at the age of twenty-six, and he is followed by the three brilliant partisan leaders, Simcoe, Tarleton, and Ferguson.

Medows and Harris must be dealt with together. In later years they both distinguished themselves in India. In America Medows commanded a battalion of grenadiers, and then gained the brilliant victory of La Vigie against the French; while the letters of Harris are most interesting.

The first eight chapters all deal with men who made their mark, and who, with the exception of Ferguson, all rose to high rank; but the letters of Lieutenant Hale are interesting just because he was not a man of note, and they describe the war from the point of view of a British subaltern.

For permission to reproduce the letters of Lieutenant Hale I am indebted to his descendant Miss Hale, and to the editor of the *Regimental Annual of the Sherwood Foresters.*

I am especially indebted to *Tarleton's History, Simcoe's Journal, the Journal of Major André, the Historical Documents* published by the Literary and Historical Society of Quebec, and Lushington's *Life of Lord Harris.*

Among modern histories of the war in America I owe a special debt of gratitude to Fortescue's *History of the British Army*, and to Major-General Greene's *Revolutionary War of the United States.* The latter work contains a wonderful series of maps.

1

Howe

William Howe, the third son of the second Viscount, was born on August 10, 1729. His father died in Barbadoes, of which island he was the Governor, in 1735, and was succeeded by his eldest son, George Augustus, who was killed near Ticonderoga in 1758. The title then passed to the second son, the famous Admiral.

William was sent to Eton, and in 1746 he received a commission in the Duke of Cumberland's Light Dragoons. He accompanied his regiment to the Continent, and took part in the campaigns of 1747 and 1748. The Duke of Cumberland's Dragoons greatly distinguished themselves at the Battle of Lauffeld on July 2, 1747, when they, together with the Greys and the Inniskillings, made a famous charge under old Ligonier, and covered the retirement of the infantry.

On the conclusion of the Peace of Aix-la-Chapelle in 1748, the Duke of Cumberland's Light Dragoons returned to England, and the regiment was disbanded at Nottingham early in 1749.

In January, 1750, young Howe was promoted captain, and six months later he was posted to the 20th Foot, in which regiment Wolfe was then a major.

In January, 1756, Howe became a major in the 58th Regiment, and in December of the following year he was promoted to the command of it. He took the 58th out from Ireland to America, and the regiment was present at the capture of Louisburg in June and July, 1758. At the conclusion of the campaign Wolfe wrote to a friend as follows:

> Our old comrade Howe is at the head of the best-trained battalion in all America, and his conduct in the last campaign corresponded entirely with the opinion we had formed of him.

In the campaign of 1759 Howe was in command of a battalion of

WILLIAM HOWE

Light Infantry. At dawn on September 13 he led "the forlorn hope" of twenty-four men of the Light Infantry who swarmed up the cliff and overpowered the picquet which guarded the path from the Anse du Foulon to the Heights of Abraham.

While the main force was landing, Howe was despatched with his Light Infantry to silence some French batteries higher up the river. During the ensuing battle he was at first posted in a wood to protect the British rear, but when the French attack developed the Light Infantry were moved up to strengthen the left flank.

On the fall of Quebec and the conclusion of the campaign, Howe resumed the command of the 58th Regiment, which remained in Quebec under General Murray. The regiment took part in the bloody battle of Sainte Foy on April 28, 1760, in which the British lost 1,000 men killed and wounded—over 30 *per cent,*—of the force engaged and were compelled to retire into Quebec. Fortunately, several British men-of-war came up the river, and the French were obliged to raise the siege and retire on May 16.

When Murray advanced on Montreal in August to co-operate with Amherst, Howe commanded a brigade of detachments, and was thus present when the final blow was delivered to the French dominion in Canada.

Soon after this Howe left America, and he commanded a brigade in the expedition to Belleisle in 1761. A landing was effected on April 22, and the citadel surrendered on June 7.

Howe was promoted colonel in 1762, and his next active service was as adjutant-general of the army that was sent to Cuba in that year. Havana was taken in August; but the mortality from disease was appalling, and by October the British had already buried over 5,000 soldiers who had died from the effects of the climate.

When peace was made in 1763, there were few young officers in the British Army who had distinguished themselves more than Colonel William Howe.

In 1764 Howe took command of the 46th Regiment in Ireland, and on June 4, 1765, he married Frances, daughter of the Right Hon. William Conolly, of Castletown, Co. Kildare.

When his brother, the third Viscount, fell at Ticonderoga, the people of Nottingham returned Colonel William Howe as their member, and he represented Nottingham in Parliament (when his military duties permitted) till 1780.

In 1772 Howe was promoted major-general, and two years later he trained "the light companies" of all the regiments at home on Salisbury Plain. At the conclusion of the training the companies were inspected by the king, and then sent back to their regiments.

At the General Election of 1774, Howe told the voters of Nottingham that if he were offered a command in a war against the Americans he should decline it.

When the war broke out, the king informed Howe that he wanted him to go to America. The general asked whether he was to consider the message as a request or an order, and he was told it was an order.

Two other major-generals were sent out at the same time—Burgoyne and Clinton; and the *Cerberus*, with the three generals on board, reached Boston on May 25, 1775.

It was natural enough that the war against the Americans should be distasteful to Howe, for his elder brother, Colonel Lord Howe, had been immensely popular with the people of New England, and the State of Massachusetts set up a memorial to him in Westminster Abbey.

When the *Cerberus* arrived an American force of some 16,000 men was investing Boston, and was extended on a front of about sixteen miles. There were two heights from which the town could be commanded—namely, Bunker's Hill and the Dorchester Heights. Recent reinforcements had brought the strength of the British Army in Boston up to 10,000 troops, so General Gage decided to occupy both these heights, and on June 12 he issued a proclamation offering a free pardon to all the rebels except a few ringleaders.

The Americans learnt Gage's intentions, and, at sunset on June 16, 1,200 men advanced to Breed's Hill, a spur at the east end of Bunker's Hill, and dug themselves in. By morning they had constructed a strong redoubt on the hill, and a trench extending from the redoubt, on the north side, for 100 yards. Gage had only to occupy Charlestown Neck to insure the surrender of the Americans on Breed's Hill, but he despised his enemy, and decided to storm the hill by a frontal attack.

Howe was selected to command the attacking force. Soon after noon two regiments were embarked, together with a battalion of grenadiers and a battalion of light infantry, and they were landed at the east end of the Charlestown peninsula. After reconnoitring the position, Howe decided to send for two more battalions. By 3 p.m. these had arrived and all was ready.

Howe briefly explained to the men that they had got to capture the hill, and added: "I shall not desire one of you to go a step farther than where I go myself." He then gave the order for the attack to commence. He himself led on the left column, and General Pigot led the right.

Meanwhile the Americans had been reinforced by 300 more men, so that they had 1,500 men on a frontage of 700 yards.

The British opened fire too soon; but the Americans reserved their fire till the enemy were within fifty yards, and then poured it in with murderous effect. After a brief struggle the British columns were shattered and fell back.

Howe at once re-formed his regiments, formed them in line, and led them the second time to the attack. Once more the assailants were broken by the murderous fire from the redoubt and trench, and fell back.

The losses had been appalling. General Clinton in Boston noticed that two battalions were in some confusion, so he jumped into a boat, hurried across, and re-formed them. In the meantime Howe had been reinforced by the 47th Regiment and two weak battalions of Marines. Several senior officers now came to the general, and urged him not to lead the men again to useless slaughter, as the hill could not be taken; but Howe quietly replied: "To be forced to give up Boston would, gentlemen, be very disagreeable to us all."

Howe had brought six field-guns over with him, but so far they had rendered no assistance; for the gunners had brought with them round shot of a size which would not fit the guns, and the artillery officers stated that, owing to a swamp, they could not advance within grape-shot range of the enemy. Moreover, in the first two attacks the infantry had advanced, weighed down with their packs and carrying three days' rations.

Howe now ordered the artillery to advance, swamp or no swamp, till they could open fire with grape. He made the infantry take off their packs, and ordered them to move forward without firing a shot, and trust to the bayonet alone. This third advance up Bunker's Hill is one of the grandest feats of arms in the history of the British Army.

Most fortunately, the ammunition of the Americans now began to run short, and they only had two or three rounds a man. Again they reserved their fire till every shot told; but the British infantry were not to be denied, and they carried the works with a rush. Hitherto the losses of the Americans had been but trifling, but as they fell back they suffered heavily from the musketry of Howe's victorious infantry, and from the guns of the fleet.

Howe's force consisted of 2,500 men, and comprised the 5th, 38th, 42nd, 47th, and 52nd Regiments, two weak battalions of marines, and the flank companies of the 4th, 10th, 18th, 22nd, 23rd, 35th, 59th, 63rd, and 65th. The casualties among the British amounted to 19 officers killed and 70 wounded, 207 N.C.O.'s and men killed, and about 850 wounded. Howe had twelve officers on his personal staff. Every one of them was shot down, and only one survived the day. The grenadier company of the 23rd went into action forty-nine strong, and at the end of the day only five men were left standing. The casualties among the British infantry came to well over 40 *per cent*, of their strength.

Over 4,000 Americans passed Charlestown Neck during the day, but their staff arrangements were bad, and, as is always the way with undisciplined troops, there was a lot of skulking, so that it is probable that not more than 1,700 men ever really fought on the hill. These raw troops fought most gallantly. They suffered severely when they were driven from their position, and they acknowledged the loss of 450 men killed and wounded.

Gage now entrenched Bunker's Hill, and held it; but he could not undertake any active operations against the Americans, because his force was absolutely devoid of any transport, and he had not even enough horses for his guns.

In September Gage was recalled to England, and Howe became commander-in-chief in the New England colonies.

As time wore on, the morale of the British troops in Boston began to suffer; fresh provisions were scarce, and sickness appeared. In November Lord George Germaine became Secretary of State for War. He was better known as Lord George Sackville, and it was under this latter name that he had rendered himself infamous at Minden. Our army has had to do with many varied types of War Ministers, but this was the only occasion on which it has had as Secretary of State for War an individual who had been tried by court-martial and dismissed from the service for misconduct in action.

Washington had to contend with grave difficulties, largely owing to the indiscipline of his men, but he was admirably supplied with information as to all that went on inside Boston.

Howe, on the other hand, could get no intelligence of the enemy, and was cooped up. He decided that Boston was useless as a base, and he meant to evacuate it as soon as more transports arrived, and when the advent of spring should give promise of fine weather. Meanwhile he could not occupy the Dorchester Heights, for he had not enough men to hold that position.

On March 2, 1776, Washington commenced a bombardment, and on the 4th the fire was kept up till late at night. After dark a large force of the enemy occupied the Dorchester Heights, and by dawn they had thoroughly entrenched themselves. Howe decided to attack these works the next night, but a storm arose and the attack could not take place.

On the 9th the Americans occupied Nook's Hill, and enfiladed the British works on Boston Neck. It was now necessary to evacuate the town, and Howe embarked his army without loss on March 17, taking with him 1,100 Loyalists. He sailed for Halifax, which port he reached on April 2.

Unfortunately, many guns and large quantities of stores had to be left behind, and in spite of Howe's orders a considerable quantity of these were not destroyed.

There was such a lack of accommodation at Halifax that Howe had to keep most of the troops from Boston on board ship. On July 11 the army left Halifax for New York. Sandy Hook was reached on June 29, and on July 3 the British landed on Staten Island about 9,000 strong. Within the next few days the convoy brought out from England by Admiral Lord Howe arrived, and the General found himself in command of an army of 25,000 men; but he was much hampered by the lack of transport and camp equipment.

General Howe had been appointed to act with his brother, the admiral, and endeavour to conciliate the Americans—in fact, as one historian puts it, the brothers were instructed to make peace if they could, and war if they must.

Howe organized his British troops into seven brigades and a reserve; he had besides two divisions of Hessians.

Washington had about 18,000 troops for the defence of New York, and, as he could not tell where Howe would strike, he was compelled to divide his forces. He kept 5,000 men in New York, and placed between 9,000 and 10,000 men under General Putnam in Long Island, to occupy an entrenched position on the Brooklyn Heights.

The attempted negotiations proved abortive, so Howe decided to strike a blow at the American force in Long Island. He landed his troops at Gravesend Bay on August 22, and spent four days in reconnoitring the enemy's position. Howe's troops were more than twice as numerous as Putnam's, but the American general was foolish enough to divide his force, and he sent forward half of it to occupy the ridge of hills which lay between the lines of Brooklyn and the British. An American detachment watched the road which skirted the western end of the hills, and the main body of the Americans, under General Sullivan, was posted across the road which led over the middle of the ridge, but the road which skirted the eastern end of the hills was neglected. Howe detected the weak point, and laid his plans accordingly.

At 9 p.m. on August 26, Clinton moved off with the reserve and the 1st Brigade to turn the American left, and Howe himself followed him with three more brigades. Thus, by soon after dawn on the 27th Howe had established himself at Bedford in rear of the American left wing. Meanwhile two brigades of Hessians made a demonstration against the American centre, and Grant threatened the right wing. The American right fought stoutly for a time, but Howe's troops quickly made their presence felt, and the remains of the American force escaped across a swamp and made their way to the fortified lines at Brooklyn, with a loss of some 2,000 men. The British captured 3 Generals, 71 other officers, 1,006 men, and 32 guns.

The troops were now anxious to storm the fortified lines of Brooklyn, but Howe forbade it.

After Bunker's Hill the Americans had said that they would be glad to let the British take some more positions at the same cost, and Howe had no intention of uselessly throwing away the lives of his men. To quote his own words:

> As it was apparent that the lines must become ours, at a very cheap rate, by regular approaches, I would not risk the loss that might have been sustained in the assault, and ordered them back to the hollow way out of the reach of the musketry.

The loss of the victors was but small, and amounted only to 5 officers killed and 16 wounded, 58 men killed and 298 wounded.

Washington came across to Long Island with reinforcements, but, finding that Howe intended to invest the lines deliberately, he embarked his whole force after nightfall on the 29th, and by 7 a.m. on the 30th he had safely withdrawn to New York.

On September 15 Howe landed his army at Kip's Bay, about three miles above New York, and took post across Manhattan Island. Washington managed to withdraw his men with the exception of about 300 who were taken prisoners; but Howe got possession of New York and took 67 guns. At this time the city had but 20,000 inhabitants, and it occupied only the south end of Manhattan Island.

The Americans who had retired towards the north were very strongly entrenched across the island. Some sharp skirmishing took place on September 16, and then there was a lull for nearly a month. Meanwhile Howe threw up works to cover New York from the north.

Early in October he decided to strike a blow at Washington's left, and threaten his communications with Connecticut.

He left three brigades to hold the recently-constructed lines, and he embarked the rest of his army on October 12. He first landed his men at a place called Throg's Neck, and then re-embarked them and landed them at Pell's Point on the 18th. Meanwhile Washington had not been idle. He changed front from south to east, and extended his army in entrenched camps behind the River Bronx.

Howe advanced with 13,000 men, and on the 25th he encamped within four miles of Washington's entrenched camp at Whiteplains. The American general occupied this camp in force, but left a detachment of 4,000 troops, under Colonel Spencer, entirely isolated, and on the other side of the River Bronx. On the 28th Howe fell upon Spencer's troops and drove them back. In this action the Royal Army lost 313 men killed and wounded, and the Americans had 140 killed.

Washington continued to strengthen his position, so Howe sent for six more battalions from New York. On November 1 Washington fell back behind the River Crotton. He left 7,000 men, under General Lee, near the Crotton, sent 3,000 to Peekskill, ordered a third detachment to Hackinsaw, and was also persuaded into holding Forts Lee and Washington on the River Hudson. The result was that he was weak everywhere.

Howe took full advantage of his opportunity. On November 15 he summoned Fort Washington to surrender, and on the following day he took it by assault. This was a crushing blow to the Americans, who lost 3,300 of their best troops killed, wounded, and prisoners, while the casualties among the British and Hessians were only 458.

Howe followed up this blow by despatching Cornwallis across the Hudson on the 18th with 1,500 men. General Greene, the American commander, was warned by a deserter, and managed to retire just in time; but all his stores and equipment fell into the hands of Cornwallis, together with Fort Lee and 140 guns. On the 24th Cornwallis advanced and pursued Washington, who had now joined Lee, to Brunswick. On December 6 Howe joined Cornwallis at Brunswick, and advanced to the Delaware. He reached Trenton on the 8th, just as the last boatload of Americans crossed the river. It was now necessary to go into winter-quarters. Howe intended to hold a line from Brunswick to Newark, but unfortunately he was persuaded to extend his front so as to include Trenton and Bordenton, for the sake of protecting the Loyalists. These two last places were occupied by Hessian troops.

Howe gave strict orders for all positions to be entrenched, but the officer commanding at Trenton neglected to obey them. On Christmas Day Washington fell upon Trenton, and the Hessians laid down their arms after a brief resistance. This successful little operation greatly inspired the Americans, and very largely destroyed the moral effect of the previous campaign.

Howe did not attempt to recover the ground he had lost, but confined himself to the position he had first selected.

We must now touch briefly on the causes which influenced the conduct of the war during the following year.

On November 30 General Howe wrote to Germaine, and reported that 35,000 troops were required for the campaign against New England, so that it would be necessary to send out 15,000 more men from home.

This letter reached London on December 30. Germaine replied that he could only send out 8,000 more troops; yet, in spite of this, he set about planning an advance on New York from Canada.

On December 20, owing to the success of his operations, Howe had changed his mind, and he now wrote advocating an advance into Pennsylvania; but on January 20 he reported that the situation had been completely altered by the reverse at Trenton.

On March 3 Germaine wrote approving the proposed campaign in Pennsylvania. He added that he could only send out 3,000 men instead of 8,000; but at the same time he recommended a "warm diversion on the coast of Massachusetts." He said not a word about operations on the Hudson, yet on the 26th he instructed Carleton to hand over 7,000 troops to Burgoyne for an advance on Albany.

On April 5 Howe wrote and told Carleton that he was about to advance into Pennsylvania, and so would not be able to co-operate with him on the Hudson.

On May 18 Germaine wrote and approved of Howe embarking his troops and taking them round for an advance on Philadelphia, and he expressed the hope that afterwards Howe would be able to assist on the Hudson.

It is thus clear that Germaine did all he could to insure the failure of the ensuing campaign.

In August, 1808, Napoleon sent to his brother King Joseph some "Observations" on the conduct of the war in Spain. After pointing out various matters of importance, he added these weighty words:

> But it is not permitted, at the distance of 300 leagues, and without even a state of the situation of the army, to direct what should be done.

The same lesson was inculcated in an amusing manner by Sir William Butler when he was commanding at Plymouth a few years ago. It had been necessary to build a canteen, and Sir William had reported that a certain site was unsuitable because of the risk of fire. His advice was disregarded. The canteen was built, and very shortly afterwards it was burnt down. When reporting the occurrence, Sir William added:

"So long as the man at a distance always knows better than the man on the spot, so long will you burn your canteens in peace and your fingers in war."

Howe received Germaine's letter of March 3 early in May, and a few weeks later some drafts arrived from England. On June 5 Howe received a copy of the instructions which had been sent to Carleton relative to the advance from Canada. No orders were sent to Howe, so he decided not to change his plans, but to enter upon the proposed operations in Pennsylvania.

By the middle of June he had withdrawn his troops to Amboy. Washington came down from the hills and advanced on Quibbletown, so Howe decided to strike at him. Early on the 26th he advanced on Quibbletown with 11,000 troops. Washington at once retired, but Howe managed to handle one detachment of the Americans very roughly, inflicting on them a loss of 250 killed and wounded, besides capturing three guns.

After this little success Howe again withdrew to Amboy, and embarked his army, which was now 15,000 strong. He waited to see Clinton, whom he was leaving in command at New York with 9,000 men. Clinton arrived on July 5, but then foul winds prevented Howe from sailing till the 23rd. The army was off Delaware Bay on July 31, but the naval officers would not undertake the responsibility of disembarking the troops in the Delaware. The force again put to sea, and it was August 25 before it landed in Elk Bay on the Chesapeake, a point only thirteen miles west of Delaware Bay.

Howe advanced slowly towards the north-east, and on September 3 his army was in touch with the Americans. On September 9 the Americans were in position on the Brandywine, and on the following day the British encamped within a few miles of them, at Kennett Square.

Washington had about 15,000 men under his command, and his position was well chosen. He held Chad's Ford strongly, and his left was covered by the river, which below the ford became an impassable torrent. The one weak point of the position was the right flank.

Howe had no superiority of numbers, but he at once detected Washington's vulnerable point, and he overthrew the Americans by a movement very similar to that which brought him victory at Brooklyn.

At dawn on September 11 Knyphausen advanced against Chad's Ford, with fifteen battalions and the bulk of the artillery, to engage the enemy's attention.

Meanwhile Cornwallis moved off to the left with seventeen battalions, and made for the upper forks of the Brandy wine.

Knyphausen drove in the American light troops, and by 10 a.m. he was able to open fire with his guns on the American main body by Chad's Ford. It was not until past noon that Washington learnt that his right flank was turned, and by 2 p.m. Cornwallis was approaching Dilworth in the right rear of the American position.

Washington now attempted a counter-attack on Knyphausen, but this was easily repulsed. He also sent a division of his army under Sullivan to oppose Cornwallis.

At 4 p.m. Cornwallis, after a march of eighteen miles, fell upon Sullivan and drove him back to Dilworth, and now Knyphausen advanced and stormed the entrenchments at Chad's Ford. Darkness saved the Americans from utter ruin, and Washington retreated, having lost 11 guns and over 1,000 men, 400 of whom had been taken prisoners. Howe only lost 8 officers and 81 men killed, 49 officers and 439 men wounded.

Howe pushed steadily forward. On the 22nd he crossed the Schuylkill and captured six guns, and on the 25th he occupied Philadelphia.

It was now necessary to make several detachments for the purpose of opening up the Delaware and bringing supplies from the Chesapeake, so that Howe's army, which was encamped at German-town, six miles north of Philadelphia, was reduced to less than 9,000 men.

Washington had received reinforcements, and on the evening of October 3 he advanced, with 8,000 regulars and 4,000 militia, to attack Howe.

The British General had full information of the advance, but he did not entrench his position, lest it should prevent the Americans from attacking him. The result of the battle proved his wisdom.

When the firing began at dawn on the 4th, Howe rode forward and met the light infantry falling back.

Thinking that the enemy were not as yet in any strength, he cried out:

For shame, Light Infantry! I never saw you retreat before. Form! Form! It is only a scouting party!

Just then the mist rolled aside and disclosed the enemy, who opened fire with several guns.

An officer of the 52nd described the situation in the following words:

I never saw people enjoy a discharge of grape before; but we all felt pleased to hear the grape rattle about the commander-in-chief s ears after he had accused the battalion of having run away from a scouting party.

Washington's plan was too complicated for his raw troops and untrained staff. His troops advanced by four different roads. At dawn there was a dense fog. The 40th Regiment occupied a house to the north of the village, and their stubborn defence entirely upset the enemy's plan. In the fog the Americans fired upon one another. Grey, finding the British left in no danger, moved across to support the threatened right flank, and Cornwallis hurried out from Philadelphia with two more battalions. After two hours and a half of sharp fighting the Americans were driven from the field, with a loss of 673 killed and wounded, besides 400 prisoners. Howe's loss was only 4 officers and 66 men killed, 27 officers and 396 men wounded, and 14 men missing.

On October 8 Admiral Lord Howe arrived with the fleet to open up the Delaware, and the general withdrew his army to Philadelphia to assist him. The Americans were finally driven from their position on the river on November 15.

Meanwhile, on October 28, Howe had written as follows to Lord George Germaine:

From the little attention, my lord, given to my recommen-
dations since the commencement of my command, I am led
to hope that I may be relieved from this very painful service,
wherein I have not the good fortune to enjoy the necessary
confidence and support of my superiors, but which I conclude
will be extended to Sir Henry Clinton, my presumptive successor. By the return of the packet I humbly request that I may
have His Majesty's permission to resign.

He had not yet learnt of the disaster of Saratoga, which drew the
following observation from Carleton:

This unfortunate event, it is to be hoped, will in future prevent Ministers from pretending to direct operations of war in a
country at 3,000 miles distance.

Germaine was, however, incorrigible, and in May, 1779, Clinton,
the new commander-in-chief, had to write to him as follows:

For God's sake, my lord, if you wish me to do anything, leave
me to myself, and let me adapt my efforts to the hourly change
of circumstances.

On December 4 Howe marched out against Washington, but he
failed to bring him to battle, so he withdrew into winter-quarters
at Philadelphia, "being unwilling to expose the troops longer to the
weather in this inclement season without tents or baggage for officers
or men."

Washington now encamped his army at Valley Forge, and his men
suffered terribly. By the end of the year he had barely 3,000 left.

Howe has been severely criticized for not attacking Washington
during the winter. In the light of after-events it seems clear that Howe
ought to have attacked, but it is only fair to remember that Grey, who
was certainly one of the best soldiers in America, stated that in his
opinion an attack upon Valley Forge would have been wholly unjus-
tifiable.

On April 14, 1779, Howe heard that his resignation was accepted.
On May 8 he handed over the command to Clinton. A few days later
he and his brother were entertained at a *fête* called a "*meschianza*" by
the officers and ladies at Philadelphia, and on the 25th he embarked
and set sail for England.

He was very popular with the army. Officers and men not only
admired him as a leader who always led them to victory, but also liked

him. His departure is described by the unfortunate André in the following words:

> I am just returned from conducting our beloved general to the water-side, and I have seen him receive a more flattering testimony of the love and attachment of his army than all the splendour of pomp of the *meschianza* could convey to him. I have seen the most gallant of our officers, and those whom I least suspected of giving such instances of their affection, shed tears while they bade him farewell.

After his return from the war, Howe frequently spoke in the House of Commons on American affairs, and, considering that the conduct of himself and his brother the admiral was impugned, in June, 1779, he got a committee of the whole House to inquire into the war.

In 1782 he was appointed Colonel-in-Second of the Royal Artillery and Royal Engineers, and Lieutenant-General of the Ordnance; and four years later he was made Colonel of the 19th Light Dragoons.

In 1789 our relations with Spain became very strained owing to the Nootka Sound incident, and Howe was appointed to command the "Spanish Armament"; but the crisis passed and war was avoided.

Howe was promoted general on October 23, 1793. When war broke out with France in that year he commanded the Northern District, with his headquarters at Newcastle, and two years later he had a force of 9,000 men in camp at Whitley, near Newcastle.

Afterwards he commanded the Eastern District, with his headquarters at Colchester.

Admiral Earl Howe died on August 5, 1799, and the general now became the fifth Viscount. In 1805 he was appointed governor of Plymouth, and he died at Plymouth, after a long and painful illness, on July 12, 1814.

Howe was a man six feet in height, and, like his famous brother "Black Dick," he was very dark. His enemies accused him, when in America, of being too fond of women, wine, and cards.

In the eighteenth century most men drank a good deal more than they do nowadays, and it seems certain that Howe was by no means a St. Antony; but it is absurd to suppose that the man who in 1758 commanded "the best-trained battalion in all America," and who in 1774 was specially selected to train the light companies of all the regiments in England, was indolent and slothful.

Surely the British Army should keep green the memory of the soldier who, as a young colonel, led the forlorn hope up the Heights of Abraham, and who sixteen years later led the British infantry to victory on Bunker's Hill!

Very few men have seen more hard fighting. As a cavalry subaltern he took part in Ligonier's famous charge at Lauffeld, and he commanded a battalion both at the Battle of Quebec and at the even more bloody battle of Sainte Foy, seven months later.

His conduct at Bunker's Hill can never be forgotten, and, when he had assumed command of the army, he beat the Americans soundly at Brooklyn, Fort Washington, Brandywine, and Germantown.

Sir William Howe understood full well that the occupation of any particular district or province should not be the chief consideration, but that the true objective should be the defeat of the enemy's army. To quote his own words:

> As my opinion has always been that the defeat of the rebel army is the surest road to peace, I invariably pursue the most probable means of forcing its commander to an action.

He was also fully alive to the folly of undertaking operations which depended for success on the co-operation of Loyalists; and he made the following statement in the House of Commons:

> In May, 1778, when I left America, 974 men constituted all the force that could be collected in Pennsylvania after the most indefatigable exertions during eight months.

Sir William Howe.

Cornet, Duke of Cumberland's Light Dragoons, September 18, 1746.

Lieutenant, Duke of Cumberland's Light Dragoons, September 21, 1747 (disbanded 1749).

Captain-Lieutenant, 20th Regiment, January 2, 1750.

Captain, 20th Regiment, June 1, 1750.

Major, 58th Regiment, January 4, 1756.

Lieutenant-Colonel, 58th Regiment, December 17, 1757.

Colonel, 58th Regiment, February 19, 1762.

Colonel, 46th Regiment, November 21, 1764.

Major-General, February 25, 1772.

Lieutenant-General, August 29, 1777.

General, October 12, 1793.

Colonel, 23rd Regiment, May 11, 1775.
Colonel, 19th Light Dragoons, April 21, 1786.
Lieutenant-General of Ordnance and Colonel-in-Second Royal Artillery and Royal Engineers, January 1, 1782.
Local General in America, January 1, 1776.

Governor of Berwick, 1795.
Governor of Plymouth, 1805.

2

Carleton

Guy Carleton, the third son of Christopher Carleton, of Newry, Co. Down, was born at Strabane on September 3, 1724.

He was gazetted an ensign in the 25th Foot in May, 1742, and promoted Lieutenant in the same regiment three years later. In July, 1751, he was transferred to the 1st Guards, and in June, 1757, he was promoted captain-lieutenant and lieutenant-colonel. Carleton was present at the capture of Louisburg in the summer of the following year, and in August he was gazetted lieutenant-colonel of the 72nd Foot. He returned home that autumn.

When Colonel James Wolfe was selected by Pitt for the command of the proposed expedition to Quebec, he chose Lieutenant-Colonel Carleton as his quartermaster-general. the king refused to sanction the appointment, as Carleton had made some disparaging remarks about Hanoverians. Wolfe protested strongly; Pitt persuaded the king to relent; and Carleton was appointed quartermaster-general in America, with the local rank of colonel, on December 30, 1758. He was wounded in the famous battle on the Heights of Abraham on September 13, 1759, and in the following year he took part in the advance to Montreal which brought the French dominion in Canada to an end.

In the spring of 1761 Carleton served as a brigadier in the expedition to Belleisle, and he was wounded in the unsuccessful attack of April 8. He was promoted colonel in February, 1762, and took part in the expedition to Havana, being wounded for the third time in a sortie which took place on July 22.

Peace was made in 1763. Many regiments were disbanded, and among others the 72nd.

Colonel Carleton was appointed lieutenant-governor of Quebec

GUY CARLETON

in September, 1766. General Murray went home on leave in the following year, so Carleton officiated as governor.

In 1771 he returned to England on leave. On May 22, 1772, he married Lady Marian, daughter of the Earl of Effingham, and three days later he was promoted major-general.

Early in 1774 he appeared before a committee of the House of Commons to give evidence in favour of the Quebec Act, which was brought forward largely at his instigation. This Act practically established the Roman Catholic Church in Canada, and restored the old French law in civil cases. Major-General Carleton returned to Quebec in the autumn, and he received a warm welcome from the Canadians. He was appointed governor of Quebec on January 10, 1775. It was a great thing at this time that the Canadians had a governor whom they liked and trusted, for in April the Revolutionary War broke out in Massachusetts.

In September, 1775, on the recall of General Gage, Sir William Howe was made commander-in-chief in the American Colonies, and Carleton was made commander-in-chief in Canada as well as governor. The situation was full of difficulty, and it was well that all power should be centred in one man.

The usual line of communications between New York and Montreal was up the Hudson, across Lake Champlain, and then down the Richelieu. This piece of country had been the scene of much desperate fighting in the old French wars. The fort of Ticonderoga, which contained eighty-seven serviceable guns and many valuable stores, was only held by a small detachment of forty-eight men. On May 8 Ethan Allan visited the fort, borrowed twenty men from the unsuspecting officer to help him in some work, made them all drunk, and then captured the fort. For the defence of the whole of Canada, Carleton had less than 1,000 soldiers, consisting of two weak battalions—the 7th and 26th Foot—and 130 gunners. In June General Gage authorized Colonel Allen Maclean to raise a regiment, to be called the Royal Highland Emigrants or 84th Foot, and Maclean succeeded in raising the first battalion in Canada by September, largely from old soldiers who had taken their discharge after the peace of 1763.

In the meanwhile the Americans had decided to invade Canada from two different points. Brigadier-General Richard Montgomery advanced from Ticonderoga on August 25, with 1,200 men and four guns, and laid siege to St. John, on the Richelieu. Montgomery was born at Swords, near Dublin, on December 2, 1736, and served for more than fifteen years in the 17th Foot. He was gazetted ensign in September, 1756, and promoted captain in May, 1762, and he sold out in 1772. He was with his regiment at Louisburg, Martinique, and Havana, and served on Haviland's staff in the advance to Montreal in 1760. After retiring he had bought a farm near New York, and when the war broke out he threw in his lot with his adopted country.

Colonel Benedict Arnold left Cambridge, Massachusetts, on September 11, with 1,050 picked men, and set out on his march through the forests of Maine.

Fort St. John, which was held by 500 British regulars and 100 Canadians, made a stout resistance, but Fort Chambly fell on October 20, and Fort St. John on November 3. Montgomery occupied Montreal on November 12, while Carleton, disguised as a fisherman, escaped down the river and passed the American batteries at Sorel in a canoe.

Arnold had reached Point Lévis, opposite Quebec, on November 10, with 650 men, after a terrible march in which 200 of his men had died in the forest, and 200 more had deserted. Many of Arnold's muskets were broken, and he had only five cartridges per man.

He was delayed for three days by a gale, but on November 13 he crossed the river, landed at Wolfe's Cove, and demanded the surrender of Quebec. Fortunately, Colonel Maclean had arrived the day before from Sorel, with some 200 men of the Royal Fusiliers and Royal Highland Emigrants. Maclean refused to surrender, and Arnold retired twenty-one miles up the river, to wait for Montgomery at Pointe aux Trembles.

The arrival of the governor is recorded in the diary of Captain Ainslie, of the British militia, in the following words:

> On the 19th (a happy day for Quebec), to the unspeakable joy of the friends of Government, and the utter dismay of the abettors of sedition and rebellion, General Carlton arrived in the *Fell*, armed ship, accompanied by an armed schooner—we saw our salvation in his presence.

The general lost no time in preparing for a vigorous defence. On November 22 he issued a proclamation that "the suspected and all who are unwilling to take up arms in its defence must leave the town within four days." On November 14 the garrison was only 1,100 strong. On November 30 it numbered 1,800 men, but of this number only 90 were British regulars, and 230 Royal Highland Emigrants, while the remainder were militia and seamen. Besides the garrison, there were 3,200 women and children in the town. There was food enough to last for eight months, though firewood, hay, and oats, were scarce. The work of strengthening the defences went on vigorously; but the walls were two miles in circumference, and required 200 men always on guard.

The attitude of the French Canadians added to Carleton's difficulties. Though but few of them joined the rebels, the remainder refused to send in supplies to the British. On December 3 one of them spread a report that 7,000 Russians were coming up the river. Carleton promptly sent him to prison "to await their arrival."

Meanwhile Montgomery had had to contend with many difficulties. His men were undisciplined ruffians, and, as he wrote to Congress, "every man a general, and not one of them a soldier." He was obliged to leave detachments at Sorel and Montreal, so that he had only 300 men available for a further advance; but realizing—to use his own words—that "till Quebec is taken Canada remains unconquered," he pushed on down the river, and joined Arnold at Pointe aux Trembles on December 3. The Americans at once advanced to Quebec. General Carleton refused to burn down the suburbs of St. Louis and St. Roche, out of pity for the owners of the houses. The Americans were thus able to approach under cover quite near to the walls, and they caused much annoyance to the defenders by shooting at the sentries.

The composition of the garrison must have caused great uneasiness to the general, for, while he might well hope that his French and British militia and seamen would stand fast behind the walls of Quebec, he could not have felt that they would have much chance against Arnold's backwoodsmen if it came to a fight in the open in anything like even numbers. Some of the general orders published during the early days of the siege are rather illuminating.

Thus, on December 14 we find:

Whoever is found drunk on guard or duty shall be confined 48 hours on bread and water, and those off duty so offending shall be confined 24 hours in like manner.

And again on December 29:

The men are not to fire their Pieces in the streets, but when necessary to have them unloaded an officer per company will attend his own men to the ramparts of the riverside between the hours of eleven and one, and will make them fire at a mark. It is recommended to the officers to confine any man who is found disobeying this order.

On the other hand, Montgomery's situation was desperate. He was 300 miles from his base, the Canadian winter was upon him, and he had barely 1,000 undisciplined men under his command; but, with splendid audacity, he decided to storm Quebec, as this offered the only possibility of success.

The Americans fell in at 2 a.m. on December 31, and the attack was delivered in a snowstorm about 5 a.m. Two small parties delivered false attacks, while Montgomery led the storming party on the south side of the town, and Arnold that on the north.

Montgomery tried to rush a stockade near Cape Diamond, but he and ten of his followers were killed at the first discharge, and the remainder fled.

Arnold was severely wounded in the leg at a stockade near the palace gate, and he was carried to the rear. His men were only opposed by some Canadian militia, and they succeeded in pushing on for some distance.

Carleton, who was in the citadel, at once sent Maclean to check Arnold's men, and another party of sixty men, under Captain Laws, to attack them in the rear. The Americans were now cut off, and 426 of them surrendered as prisoners. They had lost 20 killed and 40 wounded, while the losses of the garrison did not exceed 20 killed and wounded. By 8 a.m. the action was all over, and Quebec was saved.

Montgomery's body was identified, and buried in Quebec. In the words of one diarist:

> *January 1st.*—A genteel coffin is ordered by the lieut.-governor for the interment of Mr. Montgomery; those who knew him formerly in this place sincerely lament his late infatuation, they say he was a genteel man, and an agreeable companion.

Arnold remained the whole winter outside Quebec, but Carleton let the Canadian climate do its work while he kept his men in their quarters in the city. The British general knew well that, when the ice melted in the river, reinforcements would arrive from England, with which he could easily drive the Americans from Canada; and in the meantime he was quite satisfied to let the cold and the smallpox deal with them, and he had no intention of endangering the safety of the place by fighting another Battle of Sainte Foy.

On January 8 ninety-four of the prisoners who were captured on December 31 enlisted in the Royal Highland Emigrants to serve until

June 1. As might have been expected, the experiment was not a success, and on February 16, after ten of their number had deserted, the remaining eighty-four were disarmed and confined again.

Carleton kept the garrison fully occupied in clearing away the snow from the ramparts, getting in firewood, and other useful works. Thus we read in one diary of the siege:

January 18.—A mill wrought by horses was set going today; it makes fine flour in great quantity.

Loss of ammunition is by no means a new source of trouble. In general orders of January 26 we read:

It is the general's orders that each captain shall be answerable for the ammunition he receives for his company, and he is directed to stop four coppers per cartridge from each man who embezzles any part of his ammunition.

Nothing of any note occurred before the end of February, except that the price of food rose. Thus, beef was 7½d. a pound on January 18, but it had risen to 9d. by February 7.

During March many ingenious devices were perfected to enable the garrison to repel an attack.

An officer of the garrison writes as follows on March 4:

In the evening we threw fire balls from a mortar; they gave great light. A composition was hung over the angle at Cape Diamond; it burnt steadily and threw much light around; when it was almost consumed there were sent from it hand grenades and bullets—fragments of metal flew about in all directions.

This explosion at the end was of no use, and was afterwards omitted, but grates were fixed at the angles of all the bastions, and on March 11 we read:

Fire balls were hung over all the angles; two were lighted; they answered well; they gave great light in the ditch, and showed the faces of the bastions.

By this time 114 guns were mounted on the ramparts—none under six-pounders—besides swivels and mortars. From time to time Carleton had rockets fired at night to perplex and alarm the besiegers.

It is quaint to read in a diary of March 17:

As this was St. Patrick's day, it was expected the rebels would attack the town in hopes that a great number of the garrison would be drunk; and what confirmed us in our opinion was the junction of a great number of the enemy at their ordinary rendezvous about a mile from town. Greatly to the credit of the Irish, not a man was seen the least in liquor in the garrison.

On March 31 the only Englishman among the prisoners gave information of a plot. A large number of the prisoners had arranged to overcome their guard on the following night, seize St. John's Gate, and then set fire to three houses as a signal to the Americans, who were to march up and enter the gate. They had already managed to send word to Arnold.

Carleton determined to try to catch the enemy. In the words of one of the defenders:

> The governor, pleased with this unexpected discovery, and being possessed of the signal expected without by the enemy, immediately resolved to avail himself of the benefit derived from such information, and endeavour to decoy them within range of the ramparts, by ordering out the whole garrison under arms, at two o'clock in the morning, and every man to his alarm-post; which being accordingly done, two small brass fieldpieces were brought down to St. John's Gate, and three different fires were kindled in various directions, as if so many houses were burning; when immediately the two guns fired away, and continued repeated discharges of blank cartridge for about ten minutes.
> The garrison being now supposed to be alarmed, all the church bells were set ringing, and the drums beating; at the same time small arms were fired in various directions, while a party kept hallooing. 'Liberty, Liberty forever!' This scheme, although extremely well conducted, had not, however, unfortunately, the desired effect; for not a single man of the enemy appeared in the face of our works.

On April 1 General Wooster arrived with some reinforcements. He assumed the command of the besiegers, and opened batteries, not only on the west of the city, but also across the River St. Charles, and on Point Lévis across the St. Lawrence. His efforts were quite unavailing, and the bombardment only killed one man and one child, and wounded three men and one child.

On May 1 General Thomas assumed command of the Americans.

Next day the garrison made a sortie for firewood to the suburb of St. Louis. There they found a large number of scaling-ladders. The ladders were too short, so they were carefully left, in the hope that the Americans would make use of them. On the 3rd the enemy attempted to destroy the shipping by means of a fire-ship. On May 6 three vessels came up the St. Lawrence, and entirely cut off the Americans on Point Lévis from those across the river. Carleton landed 200 men, and then sallied out to the Plains of Abraham with 800 troops. The Americans withdrew in haste, abandoning all their stores and guns. The siege of Quebec was over, but Carleton decided to wait for his reinforcements before following up the enemy.

Ainslie wrote as follows about General Carleton:

> During the winter the general's looks were narrowly watched; the tranquillity which appeared in his countenance, added to the entire dependence we had on his military skill, dayly relieved us from former fears.

> Much strength was added to the garrison by a short but eloquent address to the militia assembled at the *château*. The substance of it was that he had the names of the disaffected in his pocket book—he well knew the friends of Government, with these he would answer with his life for the safety of the Garrison. For his part he was determined never to grace the triumph of the rebels.

On May 10 Carleton issued the following proclamation:

> Whereas I am informed that many of His Majesty's deluded subjects of the neighbouring provinces labouring under wounds and divers disorders are dispersed in the adjacent woods and parishes, and in great danger of perishing for want of proper assistance. All captain and other officers of militia are hereby commanded to make diligent search for all such distressed persons and afford them all necessary relief, and convey them to the general hospital, where proper care shall be taken of them. All reasonable expenses which shall be incurred in complying with this order shall be paid by the receiver general. And lest a consciousness of past offences should deter such miserable wretches from receiving that assistance which their distressed situation may require, I hereby make known to them that as soon as their health is restored, they shall have free liberty to

return to their respective provinces.

The disgraceful manner in which Congress behaved to Burgoyne's army in the autumn of 1777 is all the more inexcusable after Carleton's extremely generous treatment of the unfortunate Americans whom the fortune of war left in his hands.

The Americans retreated up the river to Sorel and then up the Richelieu to Chambly, where General Thomas died of smallpox on June 2.

In the meantime reinforcements had been pouring into Quebec. By June 1 Carleton had received eight British battalions and 4,300 German troops from Europe, as well as the 47th Regiment, which Howe sent from Halifax. The advance up the river was begun, and by the beginning of June Trois Rivières was occupied by a detachment under General Fraser.

On June 8 General Sullivan reached Sorel with reinforcements, and assumed command of the American Army. He had 5,000 men present, but they were utterly demoralized and dispirited, and barely 2,500 of them were fit for duty. Sullivan, however, greatly underestimated the strength of the British force, and thought he saw a favourable opportunity of striking at General Fraser's detachment at Trois Rivières, which was only twenty-five miles away. The attack was delivered on June 7 by a force of 2,000 men, but it resulted in utter failure. The Americans were routed and fled to their boats, leaving behind as prisoners a brigadier-general and 200 men. The British only had a dozen casualties.

On the 14th the British advanced from Trois Rivières, and Sullivan at once fell back by St. John and Ile-aux-Noix across Lake Champlain to Crown Point, which he reached on July 1. The invasion of Canada had proved an utter failure, and had cost the Americans 5,000 men.

On June 18 Burgoyne occupied St. John. At this point on the Richelieu River there are rapids which effectually checked the British pursuit, for the army was entirely dependent on water transport. It was also necessary to have some armed vessels, so as to insure the command of the water on Lake Champlain, which extended for seventy miles from north to south. Carleton received the greatest assistance from the navy. An eighteen-gun vessel was brought out in pieces from England and put together above the rapids. Besides this, five brigs and schooners, mounting forty-four guns between them, were built, while thirty longboats and over 400 barges were hauled up the rapids of St.

Terese and St. John. In the meantime the soldiers were thoroughly trained in wood fighting and also in rowing.

On July 6 Carleton was made a Knight of the Bath, and the king sent out the insignia by the general's wife, together with a special warrant authorizing him to wear the insignia though he had not been invested.

Busy as he was with all the preparations for an advance, Sir Guy did not forget his proclamation of May 10, and on August 7 he issued the following order:

> All prisoners from the rebellious provinces, who chuse to return home, are to hold themselves in readiness to embark on a short notice. . . . They are to look upon their respective provinces as their prison, and remain there until further enlarged.

The American troops at Crown Point were suffering terribly from smallpox and destitution. Thirty fresh graves were dug daily, and General Gates, who had assumed the command, wrote:

> Everything about this army is infected by the pestilence—the clothes, the blankets, the air, the ground they sleep upon.

In July he begged that no more reinforcements might be sent to him. One regiment, which had left New York in April 600 strong, only had five men present and fit for duty in the middle of June.

Before the end of July things were rather better, and Benedict Arnold set about the construction of a flotilla to dispute the mastery of the lake. Most of his vessels were only armed barges, which were called "*gondolas*," and they would only sail before the wind; still, their very existence rendered it impossible for Carleton to advance without armed vessels with which to overcome them. September had ended before the British flotilla was ready for action; but on October 4 Carleton advanced with 12,000 excellent soldiers in splendid condition.

The American general decided to hold Ticonderoga, and meanwhile he sent Arnold forward with his flotilla to engage the British vessels. Arnold knew that his chances of success were extremely small, and he wrote:

> I hope to be excused if with five hundred men, half naked, I should not be able to beat the enemy.

He posted his little flotilla in the narrow channel between Valcour Island and the west shore of the lake.

On the morning of the 11th the British squadron came in sight, sailed round the south-east corner of Valcour Island, and thus got between Arnold's vessels and Ticonderoga. Carleton was determined to share the dangers of his men both on land and water, so he was on the quarter-deck of the *Maria*; but he wisely left the command of the squadron in the hands of a post-captain in the navy. The larger British vessels were unable to take part in the action, which began at 12.30 p.m., and lasted for five hours; but at the end of that time the American flotilla was terribly battered. The night was misty, and Arnold managed to withdraw his flotilla unobserved; but on the 13th the British squadron again overtook him. On this occasion the *Maria* and two other vessels very soon overcame the resistance of the enemy, the American flotilla was completely destroyed, and the British remained masters of the lake.

Carleton advanced to Crown Point, which was evacuated by the enemy; but he decided to leave the capture of Ticonderoga till the following spring. The British general has been much blamed for this decision. There can be no doubt that the fall of Ticonderoga would have had a great moral effect at this juncture, and Burgoyne captured the place in four days in the following year; but, on the other hand, if Carleton had been compelled to fall back after beginning the siege, the moral effect would have been very bad. He had seen an American army perish miserably before his eyes from the effects of the climate in the previous winter; he knew that there were no more troops in England to replace the fine regiments which were with him, and he decided to keep them in good condition for the campaign of the following year, instead of attempting to carry on operations in the depth of a Canadian winter.

On November 3 the British rear-guard evacuated Crown Point, and the troops were soon in winter-quarters. Not unnaturally, there was considerable disappointment in England, and many people, who were totally ignorant of the difficulties to be overcome, loudly blamed Carleton for accomplishing so little.

Burgoyne hurried home to look after his own interests, and was in London by the middle of December. He had made himself conspicuous in the House of Commons by his attacks on Clive, and in Boston his best-known exploit was the composition of the famous proclamation which gave such offence to the Americans. Lord George Germaine disliked Carleton, and Burgoyne was well pleased to intrigue with him against his commander-in-chief.

As one observer wrote, "Burgoyne is not very communicative, and it is easy to perceive that he and Carleton were not friends."

In March, 1777, Burgoyne was appointed by the Cabinet to the command of the Northern Army for the ensuing campaign. He reached Quebec on May 6, and handed to Sir Guy Carleton detailed instructions from Germaine, specifying the precise units which were to be used in the forthcoming campaign, and announcing that the force was to be commanded by Burgoyne. On finding himself superseded in this manner, Sir Guy Carleton at once sent in his resignation, but the Ministry declined to accept it, and would not allow him to leave Canada. This was undoubtedly wise, but it was very hard on Carleton, and on July 2 the king wrote as follows to Lord North:

> Anyone that will for an instant suppose himself in the situation of Sir Guy Carleton must feel that the resigning the government of Quebec is the only dignified part. Though I think, as things were situated, the ordering him to remain in the province was a necessary measure, yet it must be owned to be mortifying to a soldier. The general seems at the same time to have facilitated as much as possible the steps necessary for enabling Burgoyne to cross the Lakes.

This praise was well earned. While the Americans at Ticonderoga were suffering terribly from smallpox and from the absence of supplies, Carleton paid careful attention to the requirements of the British troops, and practised them assiduously in wood fighting; so that when the spring came they were in first-rate condition both as regards health and discipline. Besides this, Sir Guy kept the barges and the squadron on the Lakes in excellent repair, and he used his influence with the French Canadians to get boatmen and also waggon teams for the advance on Albany.

Throughout the months of May and June Carleton exerted himself to the utmost to assist Burgoyne, with a loyalty all the more admirable when contrasted with the latter's conduct.

Burgoyne landed at Crown Point on June 27, and reached Ticonderoga four days later.

The gallantry of the commander and his troops was beyond all praise; but one cannot help feeling that the sound common-sense of Carleton, with his capacity for distinguishing between what was and what was not possible, would have avoided the disasters which culminated in the Convention of Saratoga.

No military operations took place in Canada in the year 1777, so Carleton was able to devote himself mainly to his civil duties as Governor of the province. On August 29 he was promoted Lieutenant-General.

Early in 1778 Congress planned another invasion of Canada under Lafayette; but the men of New England had no intention of restoring the French power in that quarter, so the proposed expedition came to nothing. This was fortunate for the Americans. Carleton was ready to give them a very warm reception, and the behaviour of Montgomery's men in the previous campaign had quite alienated the Canadians.

At the end of July Sir Guy Carleton left Canada on his return to England. He never again served his country in the field, and the naval action of October 13, 1776, on Lake Champlain, proved to be his last engagement. He was not a brilliant or showy general, but he was a first-rate organizer and administrator. His campaign somewhat resembled those of his old commander, Amherst, the conqueror of Canada. He always showed sound common-sense and foresight, and he left as little as possible to chance.

Sir Guy Carleton did not remain very long at home, for he was appointed commander-in-chief in America on February 23, 1782. He arrived at New York on May 5, and at once suspended hostilities, in accordance with the instructions he had received. On November 30 peace was signed between England and the United States, and the Americans left the French to make what terms they could. This was directly contrary to their treaty, but, as one of the American plenipotentiaries said, "To think of gratitude to France is one of the greatest of follies."

New York was evacuated by the British Army on November 25, 1783. Sir Guy Carleton returned home, and he was granted a pension of 1,000 a year for the lives of himself, his wife, and his two elder sons.

He was again appointed governor of Quebec on April 11, 1786, and he was raised to the peerage as Baron Dorchester in August. He arrived at Quebec on October 23 of that year.

He was appointed colonel of the 15th Light Dragoons in July, 1790, and promoted general in October, 1793.

Lord Dorchester left Quebec for the last time on July 9, 1796. He was wrecked on Anticosti Island, at the mouth of the St. Lawrence, but reached Portsmouth safely in September.

He passed the remainder of his life quietly in England, first at

Kempshot, near Basingstoke, and afterwards at Stubbings, near Maidenhead, where he died on November 10, 1808. He had a family of nine sons and two daughters, and his widow survived him till March 14, 1836.

LORD DORCHESTER (SIR GUY CARLETON).

Ensign, 25th Foot, May 21, 1742.

Lieutenant, 25th Foot, May 1, 1745.

Lieutenant, 1st Guards, July 22, 1751.

Captain-Lieutenant and Lieutenant-Colonel, June 18, 1757.

Lieutenant-Colonel, 72nd Foot, August 24, 1758.

Colonel, February 19, 1762.

Colonel, 47th Foot, April 2, 1772.

Major-General, May 25, 1772.

Lieutenant-General, August 29, 1777.

General, October 12, 1793.

Quartermaster-General in America and local Colonel, December 30, 1758.

Colonel, 15th Light Dragoons, July 16, 1790.

Colonel, 27th Light Dragoons, March 18, 1801.

Colonel, 4th Light Dragoons, August 14, 1802.

K.B., July 6, 1776.

Governor of Charlemont, January, 1777.

Baron Dorchester, August 21, 1786.

Richard Montgomery.

Ensign, 17th Foot, September 21, 1756.

Lieutenant, 17th Foot, July 10, 1759.

Captain, 17th Foot, May 6, 1762 (retired in 1772).

3

Clinton

Henry Clinton, the only son of Admiral the Hon. George Clinton, and grandson of the sixth Earl of Lincoln, was born about the year 1738. The admiral was governor of Newfoundland from 1732 to 1741, and of New York from 1741 to 1751. Young Henry became a captain-lieutenant in the New York Militia. He returned to England with his father in 1751, and on November 1 he was gazetted lieutenant in the 2nd Guards.

Henry Clinton was promoted captain and lieutenant-colonel in the 1st Guards in May, 1758, and he accompanied his regiment to Germany in the late summer of 1760, when three battalions of the Guards were sent to reinforce Prince Ferdinand. He very soon distinguished himself, and was appointed *aide-de-camp* to the Hereditary Prince of Brunswick, who commanded a division. On June 24, 1762, Clinton was promoted colonel, and on August 30 he was wounded at the action of Johannisberg, near Friedberg.

The Guards returned to England early in 1763, on the conclusion of peace. In November, 1766, Clinton was gazetted colonel of the 12th Foot, and in 1767 he married Harriett, the daughter of Mr. Thomas Carter.

Clinton was promoted major-general in May, 1772, and two months later he was returned as Member of Parliament for Boroughbridge, through the influence of the Duke of Newcastle. In 1774 he became the member for Newark, which place he continued to represent for ten years, though he was abroad most of the time.

When the trouble with the Americans came to a head, Major-General Clinton was sent out with Howe and Burgoyne. The three generals reached Boston on May 25, 1775. On June 17 Clinton saw the British infantry twice repulsed on Bunker's Hill; he then hastened

HENRY CLINTON

across the harbour, joined Howe, and led the left wing in the victorious assault. In September he was given the local rank of lieutenant-general, and on January 1, 1776, he received the local rank of general, and was appointed second-in-command to Howe.

General Clinton left Boston in December, 1775, to co-operate with the Loyalists in the South. Unfortunately, the troops were very late in arriving from England. The result was that the Carolina Loyalists were defeated at Moore's Bridge on February 27, while Cornwallis and the expeditionary force of 2,000 men did not reach the Cape Fear River till May 3. The time available for operations was now very short, as the troops were required for the New York campaign; but Clinton was determined to accomplish something, and, unluckily, he decided to capture Fort Moultrie, which commanded Charleston Harbour.

The ships were to bombard the fort while the soldiers waded across from Long Island to Sullivan Island. The information on which this plan was based proved quite unreliable; the passage between the islands was unfordable, and at the same time it was rendered impassable for boats by certain shoals. Thus the soldiers were unable to take any part in the action of June 28, and the ships were repulsed after suffering heavy loss. Clinton remained at Charleston for three weeks longer, and on July 21 he sailed for New York.

At the Battle of Brooklyn, on August 27, Clinton commanded the right column, which marched along the Jamaica road and turned the American position; and when Howe captured New York, on September 15, Clinton was in command of the first troops that landed on Manhattan Island. He accompanied Howe to Whiteplains at the end of October.

General Clinton sailed from New York with 6,000 men on December 1; he reached Newport on the 8th, and occupied Rhode Island without meeting with any resistance. The army now went into winter-quarters, and Clinton returned to England, taking with him his *aide-de-camp*, Lord Rawdon. As a reward for his services he was made a Knight of the Bath. He remained in England for some months, and did not get back to New York till July 5, 1777.

On July 23 Sir William Howe sailed for the Pennsylvanian campaign, leaving Clinton in command at New York. A week later Howe wrote to Clinton from the Delaware, and suggested that he should make a diversion on the Hudson, if he could do so without endangering the safety of New York. Burgoyne had already opened his campaign in the North, and Ticonderoga had been evacuated by the

Americans on July 5. On September 21, two days after the Battle of Bemis Heights, Burgoyne received a letter dated the 12th, in which Clinton stated that he was about to attack Fort Montgomery. Sir Henry had only 9,000 troops at New York, and he could not undertake any offensive movement till reinforcements arrived from England; but towards the end of September 3,000 recruits arrived, and on October 3 he started up the Hudson with 3.000 men.

The Americans had constructed a boom across the river three miles above Peekskill. This boom was protected by Fort Clinton and Fort Montgomery on the right bank, and also by two frigates, while four miles lower down the river, on the left bank, there was a small work at Verplanck's Point. Another work, called Fort Constitution, was situated on the left bank six miles above the boom. For the defence of these forts General Putnam had 1,200 Continental infantry, and about the same number of militia.

On October 5 Clinton seized the American work at Verplanck's Point. Thereupon Putnam withdrew some of the troops from the forts on the right bank, and retired with 2,000 men to the hills behind Peekskill. Clinton's landing on the left bank was merely a feint; at dawn on the 6th he transferred his men to Stony Point, and arranged for a simultaneous attack on Fort Clinton and Fort Montgomery. He pushed forward with his whole force till he was within a mile of Fort Clinton; then he despatched Colonel Campbell with 900 men to attack Fort Montgomery, while he himself with 1,100 assaulted Fort Clinton.

The remainder of the force was in reserve under General Tryon. The two forts had a garrison of 800 men under the command of General James Clinton, who was assisted by his brother, General George Clinton, the governor of New York. The two attacks were delivered shortly before sunset, and they were both successful.

Fort Montgomery was captured with little loss, but the Americans offered a stubborn resistance at Fort Clinton. Sir Henry had brought no guns with him, and the place was taken with the bayonet. It is rather remarkable that Fort Clinton was defended by General James Clinton, and captured by General Sir Henry Clinton. The Americans lost 100 killed and 300 captured, and the rest of the defenders made their escape. The two frigates were burnt by their crews, and the British sailors soon destroyed the boom. Sir Henry captured 67 guns in the forts, besides large quantities of powder and stores, and 30 guns were destroyed in the frigates. The British casualties amounted to 18 officers and 169 men killed and wounded.

Burgoyne had informed Clinton that he could hold out till October 12, and on the 8th Sir Henry wrote the following letter from Fort Montgomery:

> *Nous y voici*, and nothing now between us and Gates.
> I sincerely hope this little success of ours may facilitate your operations. In answer to your letter of 28th of September by C. C. (Captain Campbell), I shall only say I cannot presume to order, or even advise, for reasons obvious. I heartily wish you success.

This message, written on thin paper and concealed in a silver bullet, was sent in triplicate. One messenger (Captain Campbell) reached Burgoyne the evening before he surrendered; the second could not get through, and returned to the ships; but the third was captured and hanged as a spy, and the message fell into the hands of the enemy.

The British ships pushed up the river and destroyed Fort Constitution on the 9th; four days later a detachment under Major-General Vaughan burnt Kingston; but Clinton could do no more, and he then returned to New York.

The capture of Forts Clinton and Montgomery was an enterprise well planned and excellently carried out. Here, as at Charleston in 1780, Sir Henry showed that he could strike hard and with good effect, but one of his great merits was that he knew better than to attempt the impossible. Had he pushed on to Albany with his little force he might have shared in Burgoyne's disaster, but he could not have saved that unlucky officer; furthermore, a disaster to Clinton's force might well have endangered the safety of New York.

Sir Henry Clinton remained at New York throughout the winter. On October 22 Sir William Howe had written to Germaine asking to be relieved of his command, and pointing out that it was essential to have 10,000 more troops for the next campaign. The command was again offered to Amherst, but he declined it, and gave it as his opinion that it was impossible "to carry on with any effect an offensive land war" in America unless Howe or his successor was reinforced by 40,000 men.

Clinton was now selected to succeed to the command, and instructions for his guidance were drawn up on March 21, 1778. Clinton's difficulties were far greater than those of his predecessor, for on February 6 France had concluded a treaty with the Americans. On March 17 this was announced in Parliament, and England found herself at open war with France.

Clinton's instructions were to withdraw from Philadelphia to New York, and to send 5,000 men to attack St. Lucia, and 3,000 more to defend the posts in Florida. Thus, notwithstanding the risk of a French force appearing in North America, Clinton's force was to be reduced by 8,000 men, and he received nothing but vague promises that reinforcements would be sent during the summer.

On May 8 Sir Henry Clinton arrived at Philadelphia, and took over the command from Sir William Howe. On the 18th Washington despatched Lafayette with 2,100 men to observe the British. Lafayette advanced to Barren Hill, which was eleven miles from Valley Forge, and only two miles from the British outposts. Clinton determined to cut him off, and he very nearly succeeded. On the morning of the 19th he sent Grey and Grant to get behind the enemy, while he himself advanced against the centre. At dawn on the 20th Lafayette was almost surrounded, but he just managed to make his escape.

Clinton made no further movement before the evacuation of Philadelphia. He was fully occupied in arranging for the withdrawal of his army and of the unfortunate Pennsylvania Loyalists, who dared not remain behind. On June 18 the British Army crossed the Delaware to Gloucester Point, and marched to Haddenfield. There was an immense train of baggage, and the weather was intensely hot, so that the march of thirty-four miles to Allentown took six days. Clinton had intended to retire to Amboy, but by the 24th Washington, with 15,000 troops, had barred his path, while small parties of the enemy were busy breaking down bridges and blocking the roads.

Clinton now decided to march to Sandy Hook. Hitherto the British had been able to use parallel roads, but from Allentown to Sandy Hook there was only one road available, and the transport occupied twelve miles of road space.

Clinton now had about 15,000 men under his command. He placed Knyphausen in charge of the baggage, giving him the 17th Light Dragoons and ten battalions, while he himself covered the rear with the 16th Light Dragoons and fourteen battalions. In spite of bad roads and intense heat, the whole force reached Monmouth Court House on the 26th, and halted there next day.

On the morning of the 27th Washington, with 6,000 men, was between Cranberry and Englishtown, and Charles Lee, with 5,000 men, was at Englishtown, only six miles from Monmouth.

Knyphausen marched off with the baggage at dawn on June 28,

and Clinton followed him at 8 a.m. Washington also had marched off at sunrise, and he sent orders to Lee to attack Clinton and hold him. At 10 a.m. Lee engaged Clinton's rear-guard, but, instead of attacking with vigour, he issued orders for a retreat. The Americans thereupon fell back three miles, closely pursued by the British, till Washington, who had galloped forward to see what was happening, met them. Washington called Lee "a damned poltroon," halted the retreating troops, and took up a position with a morass on either flank. Just at this juncture his own troops arrived on the scene.

Meanwhile Clinton had taken from Knyphausen the 17th Light Dragoons and a brigade of infantry, and at 1 p.m. he assaulted Washington's position. The battle lasted for four hours in the most terrible heat. Towards sunset both sides withdrew, and took up strong positions to re-form their men. The British occupied a position about a mile and a half west of Monmouth Court House, but at 10 p.m. Clinton resumed his retreat unobserved by the enemy.

Washington marched to Whiteplains, and made no further attempt to harass the British on their march to Sandy Hook.

Clinton reported his losses in the battle as 124 dead (nearly half of them killed by the sun), 170 wounded, and 60 missing, while Washington acknowledged the loss of 58 killed, 161 wounded, and 131 missing.

During the retirement from Philadelphia the discipline of the army became seriously impaired, and some 600 men, mostly Germans, deserted. Sir Henry Clinton does not appear to have shown much skill in the Battle of Monmouth, though, as usual, he exposed himself freely and displayed great gallantry; but it was no small feat to withdraw his army in safety from Philadelphia to New York without the loss of a gun or a waggon.

Clinton's army reached New York on July 5—just in time. A French fleet of twelve ships of the line and five frigates, under D'Estaing, who brought with him 4,000 soldiers, sailed from Toulon on April 15, and arrived off the mouth of the Delaware on July 8. Three days later D'Estaing was off Sandy Hook, and he could see the British squadron under Lord Howe, which consisted of only nine ships of the line. An attack on New York was discussed, but D'Estaing was unwilling to risk his fleet in entering New York Harbour, and he decided to co-operate with General Sullivan in attacking the force of 3,000 men under Major-General Pigott, which was completely isolated on Rhode Island.

The French fleet left Sandy Hook on July 22, and was off Point

Judith just a week later. By August 8 Sullivan was in command of 2,500 Continental troops, besides 7,000 militia, and D'Estaing sailed into Narragansett Bay to co-operate with him. He was just going to land his 4,000 soldiers, when Lord Howe appeared with his squadron. D'Estaing at once put to sea, taking his soldiers with him, but a violent storm dispersed both fleets before the battle began. The British squadron was compelled to sail to New York to refit. On August 20 D'Estaing returned to Rhode Island, but on the 22nd, in spite of the protests of the American Generals, he sailed to Boston to refit, and took his soldiers with him.

Sullivan crossed to Rhode Island on August 15, and began an attack on the British redoubts; but when the French fleet sailed for Boston, the New England Militia at once deserted and returned to their homes, so that Sullivan was compelled to retreat. Pigott followed him up, and a smart engagement took place on August 29, but on the evening of the 30th the Americans withdrew to the mainland.

On the morning of the 31st the British fleet anchored in Newport Harbour, bringing with it Sir Henry Clinton and 6,000 men. Clinton had hastened to the assistance of the garrison of Rhode Island as soon as the withdrawal of the French fleet made it feasible. He was just too late to catch Sullivan, but on his way back to New York he took advantage of the opportunity to raid the little ports in Long Island Sound which harboured the American privateers, and to destroy stores and shipping.

Sir Henry Clinton found the situation intolerable, as Lord George Germaine kept constantly interfering with his plans and sending contradictory instructions; so on October 8 he wrote requesting permission to hand over the command, but his resignation was not accepted.

On November 4 D'Estaing sailed from Boston for Martinique, and Major-General Grant, with 5,000 troops, left New York for St. Lucia. Four days later Clinton despatched Colonel Campbell, with 3,000 men, to Georgia.

The winter passed quietly. The British held New York and Rhode Island. Washington dispersed his troops in a semicircle about forty miles from New York, and strengthened his position in the Highlands, making West Point the centre of his defensive works.

Clinton had not enough troops to attempt operations on a large scale, but he decided to harass the enemy by raids.

In May, 1779, Major-General Matthews visited the Chesapeake, captured Norfolk, and destroyed shipping and property worth £300,000. At the end of the month Clinton himself advanced up the Hudson, and seized the works at Stony Point and Verplanck's Point.

Washington had detached 5,000 men, under Sullivan, to deal with the Indians near the upper waters of the Delaware, so he had not enough troops for an attack on New York. He left his winter-quarters at Middlebrook and moved to West Point on July 21.

Clinton had left garrisons to hold Stony Point and Verplanck's Point, but shortly after midnight on the morning of July 16 Major-General Wayne stormed Stony Point. Washington decided not to hold the post, so it was evacuated on the 18th, and reoccupied by the British on the following day. In October Clinton withdrew the garrisons and abandoned both the posts.

Wayne's exploit was not the only American success on the Hudson, for in August "Light Horse Harry" Lee received permission to make a night attack on Paulus Hook. With 300 men he stormed the place at 3.30 a.m. on the 19th. The British lost 50 killed and wounded, and 158 taken prisoners, while Lee's casualties were only 2 killed and 3 wounded.

Meanwhile in July Clinton had sent Tyron down the Long Island Sound. He destroyed the shipping and burnt several towns, inflicting much damage. American writers are usually bitter on the subject of Clinton's raids, and seem to be of opinion that, while it was quite justifiable for the Americans to deal as harshly as they pleased with unfortunate Loyalists, the enemy ought to have treated them with every consideration. It was quite right to set fire to New York or to Portsmouth dockyard, but it appears to these writers to have been inexcusable brutality when the British retaliated in Connecticut.

On August 20 Sir Henry Clinton again wrote asking permission to hand over the command to Earl Cornwallis, who was coming out with reinforcements. Cornwallis arrived on the 25th with two new regiments and some recruits—less than 3,400 men in all. He also brought news that war with Spain was imminent, and suggestions from Germaine for an attack on New Orleans. As a matter of fact, Spain had declared war on June 16.

The Spanish government lost no time in sending the news across the Atlantic, so that the British posts of Mobile and Pensacola were captured at once.

During the autumn there was much sickness at New York. When the reinforcements arrived, 800 of them were down with fever, and six weeks later there were 6,000 men in hospital. Urgent appeals for help reached New York from the island of Jamaica, and Cornwallis was on the point of sailing with 4,000 men, when the French fleet appeared off Savannah. On October 28 Clinton withdrew the garrison from Rhode Island, and made his arrangements for a campaign in Carolina as soon as the departure of the French fleet should enable him to transport his army to the South.

On October 20 D'Estaing, having been repulsed at Savannah, sailed for France. Clinton received the news in the middle of November, and he was now free to move. On December 1 the army at New York was rather over 28,000 strong, and consisted of 13,800 British Regulars, 10,800 Hessians, and 4,000 Provincials. New York required a garrison of 15,000 men for its defence, so the force available for extensive operations elsewhere was perilously small. The operations in Georgia had been very successful, and the Ministry at home were most anxious for the conquest of the Southern States.

On December 26 Clinton sailed with 7,600 men, leaving Knyphausen in command at New York. The voyage was very stormy, and the transports only began to arrive at Tybee Island towards the end of January, 1780. From Tybee, Clinton sailed to the mouth of the Edisto on February 11, and thence he advanced across the chain of islands to Charleston. It was March 29 before the British crossed the Ashley River and opened the first parallel at 1,800 yards. This delay had given General Lincoln ample time to strengthen his defences and to call up reinforcements, till he found himself at the head of a garrison of 7,000 men. As events turned out, this was most fortunate for the British.

The siege went on in due form. On April 12 Tarleton surprised General Huger at Biggin's Bridge, and severed the American communications with the North. On the 26th Lord Rawdon arrived from New York with 2,500 men, and was placed in command of the troops on the left bank of the Cowper River. On May 6 the third parallel was opened at 200 yards, and Fort Moultrie was captured by the sailors. On the 8th the British drained the canal in front of the American works, and on the 12th General Lincoln surrendered. The fall of Charleston was a great disaster to the Americans. Their losses during the siege had only amounted to 92 killed and 146 wounded, but 5,500 officers and men became prisoners of war, as well as 1,000 sailors. The British also captured 391 guns and over 5,000 muskets, besides 17 colours and large quantities of stores and ammunition.

The British casualties during the siege were only 76 killed and

179 wounded—a trifling price to pay for so great a prize. This brilliant success, on the very scene of his former failure, must have been peculiarly gratifying to Sir Henry Clinton.

The British army in the South was about 12,500 strong, but already the dangers of carrying on war in two widely separated parts of America were apparent. The French fleet might be expected to return at any time, so Clinton was obliged to hasten back to New York with 4,000 men, leaving Cornwallis with the remainder to complete the conquest of the Carolinas.

Clinton left Charleston on June 5, and reached New York on the 17th. A few days before this Knyphausen had conducted an expedition to Springfield, and then retired very hastily. On his arrival Clinton sent Knyphausen up to Springfield again with 5,000 men, while he embarked a portion of his army as if to move up the Hudson.

On July 10 a French fleet of seven ships of the line and three frigates, escorting 6,000 soldiers under Rochambeau, reached Rhode Island. The French soldiers were to be under the orders of Washington, and he sent Lafayette to arrange with Rochambeau for an immediate attack on New York. This plan came to nothing. The other 4,000 troops who were destined for the expedition were blockaded in Brest Harbour, and on July 13 Admiral Graves reached New York with six ships of the line, which restored the command of the sea to the British.

Clinton arranged with Arbuthnot, who commanded the fleet, for a joint attack on the French in Rhode Island. On July 27 he embarked with 6,000 men and entered the Long Island Sound, but he was compelled to return to New York on the 31st, in consequence of friction with the admirals, and also because Washington advanced and threatened King's Bridge. The fleet sailed to Rhode Island, and blockaded the French so effectively that they were unable to leave the island for seven months.

The American general Benedict Arnold had for some months past been carrying on an anonymous correspondence with the British headquarters. The officer who conducted the negotiations at New York was Major André, who had been *aide-de-camp* to Grey and then to Clinton, and who, young as he was, had been appointed by the latter adjutant-general of the army in America. Arnold was in command at Philadelphia after the British troops were with-drawn, and while there he got into debt. He was tried by court-martial, found guilty on two trivial charges, and sentenced to be reprimanded. He begged

Washington to put him in command of the defences of the Hudson, which centred in West Point; Washington granted his request, and on August 4 he assumed the command. Arnold now proposed to betray West Point. On September 16 Rodney reached New York from the West Indies, and on the 18th Washington went to consult Rochambeau in Rhode Island.

Taking advantage of this opportunity, Arnold suggested that an officer should be sent to arrange with him about West Point. Clinton sent André, and gave him particular instructions that he was to wear uniform. The meeting took place after dark on the 21st, near Crown Point, and Arnold gave André various papers, some of which were in his own handwriting. As ill-luck would have it, an American battery opened fire on the frigate which was waiting for André, and compelled it to drop down the river. André was thus obliged to disguise himself, but he was furnished with a guide and a safe-conduct by Arnold. He had almost regained the British lines, when he was seized by some armed men. Thinking they were Loyalists, he announced that he was a British officer; he was thereupon searched, and the papers were found in his boots.

André was tried by a court-martial, and sentenced to death as a spy. Clinton wrote to Washington, and did all he could to save his staff officer. The sentence of the court-martial was undoubtedly just, and Washington cannot be blamed for confirming it; but it is much to be regretted that he should have allowed a communication in the handwriting of his secretary, Hamilton, to be sent to Clinton intimating that the only way to save André was to hand over Arnold. The British general, naturally, treated the suggestion with the contempt it deserved. It is said that Arnold went to him and offered to take Andre's place, but Clinton would not allow it. André was hanged on October 2. Shortly before his death he wrote to Clinton, stating that he himself was responsible for his own death, because he did not wear uniform, though he had received explicit orders to do so, and begging Sir Henry not to feel that it was in any way his fault.

Cornwallis had written in August urging Clinton to make a diversion on the Chesapeake to assist him in the Carolinas. The discovery of Arnold's treason put an end to the attempt on West Point, so on October 16 Clinton despatched Major-General Leslie with 2,500 men, giving him orders to destroy the American magazines at Petersburg, and then to get into touch with Cornwallis. On his arrival in the Chesapeake, Leslie received a letter from Lord Rawdon requesting him to bring his detachment at once to the Cape Fear River, and in due course he joined Cornwallis. The latter had begun an advance into North Carolina, but the defeat and death of Ferguson, on October 7, had upset all his plans, and he had fallen back to Winnsboro.

Arnold, who was now a brigadier-general in the British service, urged Clinton to concentrate his army, and employ it as a whole either against Washington on the Hudson or else in the South; but Germaine insisted on the British forces being scattered broadcast in a manner which insured disaster if the British should lose command of the sea.

When Clinton heard that Leslie had sailed to Charleston, he despatched Arnold to the Chesapeake with 1,600 men to make a diversion, as requested by Cornwallis.

The general outlook was now very gloomy for England. Russia, Denmark, and Sweden, had formed an agreement called the "Armed Neutrality," which was aimed at England; and on December 20 England was compelled to declare war against Holland, in consequence of flagrant breaches of neutrality by the Dutch. Thus, at the end of the year 1780, England, besides fighting the Americans, found herself at war with France, Spain, and Holland—the three strongest naval powers in Europe.

We must now turn to the theatre of war in the South. Till the close of the year 1780 Earl Cornwallis had worked loyally with Sir Henry Clinton, but in December his *aide-de-camp*, Captain Ross, of the 45th Foot, who had been sent home with the Camden Despatches, rejoined him, and from that time on his attitude towards Clinton changed.

One might have hoped that, after his unfortunate experience with Burgoyne, even Germaine would not have again encouraged a junior officer to be disloyal to his commander-in-chief; but he was not cured till his folly, meddling interference, and encouragement of disloyalty to the commanders in America, had brought about Yorktown as well as Saratoga.

After the Battle of Guildford, on March 15, 1781, Cornwallis retreated to Wilmington. Greene only pursued him to Deep River, and then decided to recover South Carolina.

Cornwallis had received instructions to subjugate the whole of the Carolinas if he could, but at any rate to hold what he had got, and particularly not to risk the loss of Charleston. So far from obeying these orders, he had caused the fortifications of Charleston to be partially levelled, and on April 25 he abandoned South Carolina to its fate, and set out from Wilmington on a march of 200 miles to Virginia.

Clinton first heard reports of this march in the middle of May, and on the 18th he wrote:

I hope Cornwallis may have gone back to Carolina. . . . If he joins Phillips I shall tremble for every post except Charleston, and even for Georgia.

The winter passed quietly in the North. Clinton had not enough troops to undertake active operations in that quarter, and Washington was beset by many difficulties. There were two serious mutinies in the American Army during the month of January, 1781. Clothing, food, and powder, were all badly needed, the men were in a pitiable state, and the paper money, which was already quoted at 1,000 dollars to one of specie, was now absolutely valueless.

On April 4, when the war had been in progress six years, Washington wrote:

If France delays timely aid now, it will avail us nothing if she attempt it hereafter. . . . We are at the end of our tether, and now or never our deliverance must come.

Meanwhile, on March 12, the French fleet and army at last left Rhode Island and sailed for the Chesapeake to crush Arnold. Fortunately, the British fleet reached the Chesapeake in time, and compelled the French to return to Rhode Island. On the 26th Clinton despatched Major-General Phillips, with 2,600 men, to join Arnold and assume the command of the combined force, and two months later he despatched another reinforcement of 1,500 men to join Phillips. In six months Clinton sent 5,700 men to Virginia.

Towards the end of May, Washington and Rochambeau planned an attack on New York, and Washington wrote to De Grasse urging him to bring his fleet and as many soldiers as he could. A letter from Washington to Lafayette mentioning this project fell into Clinton's hands. Clinton thereupon sent the letter to Cornwallis, and ordered him to send part of his force back to New York as soon as possible, and to fortify a post on the Chesapeake as a base for future operations.

On June 11 Clinton wrote as follows:

By the intercepted letters, enclosed to your lordship in my last despatch, you will observe that I am threatened with a siege in this post. My present effective force is only ten thousand nine hundred and thirty one. With respect to that the enemy may collect for such an object, it is probable they may amount to at least twenty thousand, besides reinforcements to the French (which from pretty good authority I have reason to expect) and the numerous militia of the five neighbouring provinces.

Cornwallis received these instructions at Williamsburg on June 26. He crossed the James River, and on July 8 he received further instructions to send off 3,000 men for the purpose of destroying the enemy's stores at Philadelphia. Meanwhile Germaine had written on May 2 forbidding Clinton to withdraw a single soldier from the Chesapeake; so, on receipt of this order, Clinton wrote to Cornwallis and told him he might keep all his men, adding that both he and the admiral considered a fortified post on the Chesapeake essential. Cornwallis chose Yorktown and Gloucester for the purpose, and concentrated his force there by August 22.

Meanwhile, on July 6, Rochambeau, with 4,700 French soldiers from Rhode Island, joined Washington at Whiteplains. The allies threatened New York, and towards the end of the month Washington reconnoitred Fort Lee and the lines at the northern end of Manhattan Island, but he found them too strong to attack.

Clinton knew that De Grasse was expected from the West Indies. Early in August he received a reinforcement of 2,500 Hessians, and when the British fleet returned, on the 16th, he urged Graves, who had succeeded Arbuthnot in the command, to join him in an immediate attack on Rhode Island, but the admiral would not entertain the idea.

On August 21 Washington crossed the Hudson to Stony Point, and marched southward as if to threaten Staten Island. The movement was very cleverly executed, and it was September 2 when Clinton wrote the following letter:

My Lord,
By intelligence which I have this day received, it would seem that Mr. Washington is moving an army to the southward, with an appearance of haste, and gives out that he expects the co-operation of a considerable French armament. Your lordship, however, may be assured that, if this shall be the case, I shall either endeavour to reinforce the army under your command by all the means within the compass of my power, or make every possible diversion in your favour.

Cornwallis received the letter on the 15th.
When Clinton wrote this letter he had no special cause for anxi-

ety, for he had no reason to suppose that the British fleet would for the time being lose the command of the sea. By the 6th he had heard that De Grasse was in the Chesapeake, and he wrote as follows to Cornwallis:

> As I find by your letters that De Grasse has got into the Chesapeake, and I can have no doubt that Washington is moving with at least six thousand French and rebel troops against you, I think the best way to relieve you is to join you, as soon as possible, with all the force that can be spared from hence, which is about four thousand men. They are already embarked, and will proceed the instant I receive information from the admiral that we may venture, or that from other intelligence the commodore and I shall judge sufficient to move upon.

A few days later the British fleet returned to New York to refit, after an indecisive action with the French off the mouth of the Chesapeake. Cornwallis received this last letter on the 16th, and at once replied as follows:

> If I had no hope of relief, I would rather risk an action than defend my half-finished works; but as you say Digby is hourly expected, and promise every exertion to assist me, 1 do not think myself justified in putting the fate of the war to so desperate an attempt.
> . . . Lieutenant Conway of the *Cormorant* is just exchanged. He assures me that, since the Rhode Island squadron has joined, they have thirty-six sail of the line. This place is in no state of defence. If you cannot relieve me very soon, you must be prepared to hear the worst.

It is very hard to understand the behaviour of Cornwallis. His letter proves that he knew the French were in such overwhelming strength that at the best the result of a naval action must be extremely doubtful. His force was far stronger than Lafayette's, yet he made no attempt to crush Lafayette before he was reinforced. On the 14th General Washington arrived, but his troops did not begin to arrive for some days, and it was the 26th before the allied army of 16,000 men was concentrated and ready to commence operations. If Cornwallis did not care to attack Lafayette, he might have retired to South Carolina. The disaster would at least have been far less complete than that which he brought about by attempting to hold "half-finished works."

The allies appeared before Yorktown on September 28. Next day Cornwallis received a letter stating that Clinton hoped to sail with 5,000 troops and twenty-six sail of the line on October 5.

On receipt of this letter Cornwallis at once abandoned his outer line of works, and fell back to his second line, which was commanded by the works he had given up.

On October 17 Cornwallis entered into negotiations with Washington, and on the 19th he capitulated.

The British fleet took a long time to refit, and it was October 19 before Clinton sailed with 7,000 men. He reached the mouth of the Chesapeake on the 24th, only to find that he was too late. There was nothing to be done except return to New York.

Cornwallis surrendered with 7,100 soldiers and 840 sailors. If he had not abandoned his outer line of defence before a shot was fired, there can be little doubt that he could have held out till Clinton reached the Chesapeake. Cornwallis would not have been in Virginia at all if he had not abandoned Carolina in defiance of his orders. He had neglected either to attack Lafayette or to retire while there was yet time, and by withdrawing from his line of redoubts he had at all events hastened the disaster. In spite of all this, he wrote as follows to Sir Henry Clinton on the day after the capitulation:

I never saw this post in a very favourable light. But when I found I was to be attacked in it in so unprepared a state by so powerful an army and artillery, nothing but the hopes of relief would have induced me to attempt its defence; for I would either have endeavoured to escape to New York by rapid marches from the Gloucester side, immediately on the arrival of General Washington's troops at Williamsburg, or I would, notwithstanding the disparity of numbers, have attacked them in the open field, where it might have been just possible that fortune would have favoured the gallantry of the handful of troops under my command. But, being assured by your Excellency's letters that every possible means would be tried by the navy and army to relieve us, I could not think myself at liberty to venture upon either of these desperate attempts.

A successful defence, however, in our situation was perhaps impossible; for the place could only be reckoned an entrenched camp, subject in most places to enfilade, and the ground, in general, so disadvantageous that nothing but the necessity of fortifying it as a post to protect the navy could have induced any person to erect works upon it.

The fall of Yorktown brought all active operations in America to a close. Sir Guy Carleton arrived at New York on May 5, 1782, and took over the command. Sir Henry Clinton returned at once to England.

Clinton commanded the army in America for just four years. It was his misfortune to succeed Sir William Howe, a general who was immensely popular with his troops, and who had won a brilliant series of victories in the field. Sir Henry Clinton never showed that he possessed the tactical ability of his predecessor, and during the whole period of his command he only fought one general action in the field against the enemy—the indecisive battle of Monmouth Court House, on June 27, 1778. Though he did not prove himself a brilliant leader, he showed at Fort Clinton and at Charleston that he could strike hard and skilfully. His policy of raids very nearly achieved success by exhausting the enemy, and his sound common-sense saved him from undertaking many foolish projects suggested by Germaine at home and by Loyalists in America.

Above all, he fully recognized that the command of the sea was absolutely essential to success. When Washington sent Colonel Laurens on a mission to France in January, 1781, he told him to point out that the two things absolutely necessary were a loan, and "a constant naval superiority" in American waters. Clinton recognized the truth of this. It was very hard for him to carry on the war successfully when he had no control at all over the navy, on which the success or failure of all military operations ultimately depended. Much might have been achieved had there been the same loyal co-operation between the two services as there was between Grey and Jervis in the West Indies in 1794; but so great was the friction between Clinton and Admirals Arbuthnot and Graves that the general was obliged to organize his own service of despatch vessels to keep up communications with Cornwallis.

In 1788 Sir Henry Clinton published a narrative of the operations in America. This was answered by Cornwallis, and the controversy went on till Clinton's death. The pamphlets written by the two generals, together with their official correspondence, were collected by Mr. B. F. Steevens, and published in two volumes in 1888.

General Clinton never went on active service again after his return from America. In 1790 he was elected Member of Parliament for Launceston. Sir Henry was promoted general in October, 1793, and he was appointed governor of Gibraltar in July, 1794. He died at Gibraltar on December 23, 1795.

He left two sons, who in due course became General Sir Henry Clinton, G.C.B., and General Sir William Henry Clinton, G.C.B.

Sir Henry Clinton.

Lieutenant, 2nd Foot Guards, November 1, 1751.
Captain and Lieutenant-Colonel, 1st Foot Guards, May 6, 1758.
Colonel, June 24, 1762.
Colonel, 12th Foot, November 28, 1766.
Major-General, May 25, 1772.
Lieutenant-General, August 29, 1777.
General, October 12, 1793.

Local Lieutenant-General, September 1, 1775.
Local General, January 1, 1776.
Colonel, 84th Foot, December 16, 1778.
Colonel, 7th Light Dragoons, April 21, 1779.

4

Rawdon

Francis Rawdon, the eldest son of John, Lord Rawdon, by his third wife, Lady Elizabeth Hastings, was born on December 9, 1754. From the year 1761 he was known by the courtesy title of Lord Rawdon.

He was educated at Harrow. In August, 1771, he was gazetted as an Ensign in the 15th Foot, but he seems not to have joined the regiment, and in October of the same year he matriculated at University College, Oxford. He did not take a degree. In October, 1773, he was promoted lieutenant into the 5th Foot, and he went to America with the regiment, which embarked at Monkstown, near Cork, on May 7, 1774, and landed at Boston in July.

The grenadier company of the 5th was present at the action of Lexington on April 19, 1775. The company was commanded by Captain Harris, who afterwards became Lord Harris of Seringapatam. Young Rawdon was now posted to the company in place of the subaltern who was wounded at Lexington, and served with it at Bunker's Hill on June 17. It was here that he first made his mark. He was not hit, but two bullets passed through his hat. After the fall of Harris he led the grenadiers, and greatly distinguished himself. General Burgoyne wrote:

> Lord Rawdon has this day stamped his fame for life.

In the following month he was promoted Captain into the 63rd Foot. During the weary investment which followed the Battle of Bunker's Hill, various entertainments were organized to keep up the spirits of the garrison of Boston. At one of these we find that the prologue was spoken by Lord Rawdon. In like manner during the Peninsular War the officers of the light division were adepts at theatricals.

Soon after this Rawdon was appointed *aide-de-camp* to General

FRANCIS RAWDON

Clinton, and he was present with that officer at the Battle of Brooklyn in August, 1776. He was next present at the Battle of White-plains, and at the capture of Fort Washington and Fort Lee, and he was with Cornwallis on his march through New Jersey to the River Delaware in December, 1776.

Immediately afterwards he came home with General Clinton, and in the early spring of 1777 he met Lafayette at a ball in London. He returned to America with the general, and in October Clinton sent him to Pennsylvania with the despatches reporting the capture of Fort Clinton and Fort Montgomery. He reached Sir William Howe's headquarters on October 17, and he did not return to New York. At Philadelphia he raised a provincial regiment which was known as the "Volunteers of Ireland." This corps was formed entirely of Irish deserters from the American Army. It distinguished itself greatly at Camden and Hobkirk's Hill.

At first there was a great number of desertions, but Rawdon soon put an end to this in an effective, though somewhat irregular, manner. One of the deserters was apprehended. Lord Rawdon formed up the battalion, and had the man brought on to parade. He then handed the deserter over to be tried and punished by his comrades. All the officers left the parade-ground. The man was promptly hanged on the nearest tree, and there was no more trouble of this sort in the regiment.

When Philadelphia was evacuated in the following year, Rawdon's regiment received its baptism of fire in the action of Monmouth Court House on June 28. After this Washington made no further attempt to interfere with Clinton's retreat, and the British troops reached Sandy Hook, and were sent across to New York.

Meanwhile, on June 15, Rawdon had been promoted Lieutenant-Colonel, and appointed adjutant-general of the army in America.

After the return to New York there were no more operations on a big scale in the Northern States, and the year 1779 was an uneventful one as far as Rawdon was concerned. On December 26 Clinton sailed for Charleston with a force of 7,600 men. Rawdon remained at New York, where Knyphausen was left in command.

Clinton opened his first parallel against Charleston on March 29. Meanwhile he had sent to New York for reinforcements, and on April 18 Lord Rawdon arrived with 2,500 men.

Rawdon was put in command of the force operating on the left bank of the Cooper River. On April 24 he captured the works on Haddrell's Point. On May 6 Fort Moultrie surrendered, and six days later a capitulation was signed, and Charleston fell into the hands of the British.

Clinton arranged for three columns to march on Camden, Ninety-Six, and Augusta, and on June 5 he himself sailed for New York with 4,000 men, leaving Cornwallis with the remainder to subjugate the South. Fierce guerilla warfare broke out in South Carolina between the Loyalists and the rebels, and a brilliant partisan leader named Sumter quickly made himself conspicuous by his attacks on the British posts. Meanwhile Gates reached Hillsborough on July 25, and on the following day he started to march on Camden, where Rawdon was in command. Rawdon knew of the American advance, so he moved forward with four weak battalions to Lynch's Creek, fifteen miles north-east of Camden, to cover the retirement of his outlying detachments. Having accomplished his object, Rawdon fell back on Camden.

On August 10 Gates reached Lynch's Post, and on the 13th he moved to Rugeley's Mills, thirteen miles north of Camden. Gates believed that he had 7,000 available troops, but on August 14 he was informed that he only had 3,052 present fit for duty. It is amusing to note that he had thirteen generals with this force.

On this same morning Cornwallis arrived at Camden. He decided to attack the Americans at once, for a retirement would mean abandoning 800 sick and large quantities of stores. The morning state of the British force shows 122 officers and 2,117 men present fit for duty. Cornwallis formed his army into two brigades, a brigade of regulars, under Colonel Webster, consisting of three companies of Light Infantry, the 23rd, and the 33rd; and a brigade of provincials, under Lord Rawdon, formed by the Volunteers of Ireland, the infantry of Tarleton's legion, and another colonial corps.

By a strange coincidence, each general set his army in motion at 10 p.m. on August 15, intending to surprise his opponent. The advance-guards met about 2 a.m. nine miles north of Camden. The Americans were driven back, but Cornwallis decided to wait for dawn before he attacked.

The American Army had suffered greatly from the heat. On the afternoon of the 10th the soldiers were given a heavy meal of corn-meal and meat, together with a gill of molasses. The result was that during the night march they suffered severely from acute diarrhoea, an unromantic but very weakening complaint.

Gates drew up his army with a brigade of regulars on his right and a brigade of militia on his left.

Cornwallis placed Webster on the right and Rawdon on the left; in reserve he kept two battalions of Fraser's Highlanders and Tarleton's Cavalry.

At dawn Webster fell upon the American Militia, and they at once broke and fled. The American Reserve attempted a counter-attack, but this was repulsed. Webster then wheeled to the left and fell upon the flank of the American Regulars, who were stoutly opposing Rawdon. At the same time Tarleton swept round and fell upon their rear. The American Regulars had fought well for nearly an hour, but they now broke and fled.

Cornwallis lost 20 officers and 304 men killed and wounded. The Americans lost about 1,000 killed and wounded, while over 1,000 prisoners were taken, together with seven guns and all their baggage and stores. Ten days after the battle only 700 men could be assembled at Hillsborough.

Cornwallis, having decided to advance into North Carolina, set out from Camden on September 7, but he did not reach Charlotte till the 22nd.

Guerilla warfare had again broken out in South Carolina, and on October 7 Major Ferguson was killed and his force destroyed by American backwoodsmen at King's Mountain.

Cornwallis now made up his mind to retire, and he fell back to Winnsboro. During the retreat he was taken ill, and the command devolved on Lord Rawdon.

In this campaign, as so often is the case, the difficulties of the commanders were largely increased by the inaccuracy of the maps at their disposal, and on October 23 Rawdon wrote to Colonel Tarleton as follows:

> I am very much obliged to you, my dear sir, for the pains which you have taken in looking out for a position for us. All the maps of the country which I have are so very inaccurate that I must depend totally on your judgement.

On October 24 Rawdon received a letter from Clinton saying that Colonel Leslie, with 2,500 men, had sailed for the Chesapeake to act under Cornwallis. Rawdon at once wrote and asked Leslie to come on by sea to the Cape Fear River. Soon after this Cornwallis resumed the command.

The war had been waged with a good deal of ferocity in Carolina by the irregular partisans of both sides, and the British had captured in arms a considerable number of Americans who had given their parole. Some of them were tried and executed. In October, 1780, Washington wrote to Clinton and complained of the undue severity displayed by Cornwallis and Rawdon. When Rawdon heard of this, he wrote:

> The rebels have, by the rigour of their administration, reaped too many advantages over our forbearance to wish that we should affect more energy.

For the next two months the main body of the British remained Dear Winnsboro, but the troops on the lines of communication were much harassed by the American partisans.

On January 7, 1781, Cornwallis again advanced towards the North with a force which, when Leslie had joined him, amounted to 4,000 men.

Tarleton was defeated at the Cowpens on January 17, and Cornwallis, after pursuing Greene to the Dan without bringing him to action, fell back to Hillsborough on February 20. Greene now advanced to Guildford, twelve miles north of Hillsborough. On March 15 Cornwallis advanced with 2,000 men and attacked Greene, who had 4,300 soldiers under arms.

The attack was successful and the Americans were driven from the field; but it was a Pyrrhic victory, for Cornwallis was so weakened by his losses that he had no alternative but to retreat. Instead of falling back on Camden, he retired down the Cape Fear River, and reached Wilmington on April 7.

On April 25 Cornwallis definitely abandoned the South, and set out on a march of 200 miles to Virginia—a movement which was destined to end disastrously at Yorktown. Cornwallis acted in this reckless manner entirely on his own initiative, and without waiting for orders or instructions from Clinton. He left the troops in the South in a very critical situation, for, in the words of Tarleton:

> The communications were so entirely cut off that Lord Rawdon had no manner of knowledge of the movements of the British Army after the Battle of Guildford.

When Cornwallis advanced in January, he left Rawdon to hold the South with five regular battalions and ten provincial corps. This force amounted to about 8,000 men; but, apart from the garrisons of Charleston and Savannah, there were only about 3,500 men available, and even these were much scattered. Rawdon was at Camden with 1,400 men, and he had posts at Augusta, Ninety-Six, Fort Granby, Orangeburg, Fort Motte, Fort Watson, and Georgetown.

When Cornwallis retired down the Cape Fear River and uncovered the South, Greene at once decided to march on South Carolina. Greene himself marched on Camden with his main body. He ordered Henry Lee, the father of the illustrious Confederate general, to move on his left flank, watch Cornwallis, and then to join Marion and attack Fort Watson. He despatched another force under Pickens to attack Ninety-Six.

Greene reached Camden on April 20, but, considering Rawdon too strong to attack, he fell back two miles to Hobkirk's Hill.

Three days later Marion and Lee captured Fort Watson with its garrison of 120 men. The siege lasted eight days, and the place was taken by the besiegers constructing in the night a tower of timber which completely overlooked the defences.

Rawdon had 900 men at Camden. Greene's force consisted of 1,174 regulars and 248 militia. He decided to wait for Marion before attacking. Rawdon knew that Greene would soon receive reinforcements, so he decided to assume the offensive at once. At 9 a.m. on April 25 he marched with 800 men to attack Greene. He made a detour through the woods, and approached the American position from the south-east, where the ground was less steep.

The British force consisted of the 63rd Foot and three provincial corps—the New York Volunteers, the King's Americans, and the Volunteers of Ireland. There were also a few Carolina Militia and about sixty provincial Dragoons.

Rawdon advanced to the attack with the 63rd Foot on the right, the New York Volunteers in the centre, and the King's Americans on the left. He placed some colonial marksmen on either flank to pick off the American officers. In support he kept the Volunteers of Ireland and a party of convalescents. In rear of all were the sixty dragoons.

Greene had drawn up his men with two Virginia regiments on the right, and the two famous Maryland regiments on the left. In the centre he placed his two guns. He kept his militia and his cavalry in reserve.

The action began at 10 a.m. As the British advanced, Greene ordered his two flank battalions to turn inwards and envelope the British line. Rawdon at once brought up his supports, the Volunteers of Ireland on the right and the convalescents on the left, and thus caught both these counter-attacks in flank.

Meanwhile some of the American officers had been picked off by the colonial skirmishers. The Maryland regiments now broke and fled, and Greene gave the order to retreat. He saved his guns, and took up another position five miles in rear. Greene returned his losses as 19 killed, 115 wounded, and 136 missing. He was much depressed, and on May 10 wrote to the French minister:

> We fight, get beat, rise and fight again.

The British casualties amounted to 13 officers and 245 men killed, wounded, and missing.

Rawdon had captured 100 prisoners, but the chief use of his victory was that it gave him time to concentrate. Cornwallis described the victory of Hobkirk's Hill as "by far the most splendid of this war." It was certainly a very brilliant achievement for a young officer of twenty-six to attack an enemy whose force exceeded his own by more than 50 *per cent.*, and drive him from his chosen position.

At the time of the battle Pickens was approaching Ninety-Six, and Marion and Lee were in the Santee Hills.

On May 7 Rawdon received a reinforcement of 500 men. Greene fell back to Rugeley's Mills, but sent Lee against Fort Granby, and Marion against Fort Motte. Rawdon had no alternative but to retreat. He evacuated Camden on May 9, and reached Monck's Corner (thirty miles from Charleston) on the 24th.

The Americans were not slow to seize this opportunity. On May 12 Marion captured Fort Motte. The post was held by 150 men. The enemy managed to set the roof on fire by means of burning arrows.

Rawdon had ordered Orangeburg to be evacuated, but before anything was done Sumter appeared and captured the place, with its garrison of 350 men, on May 11.

Four days later Lee took Fort Granby, which was held by 240 men. All the inland posts had now fallen except Ninety-Six and Augusta.

Things looked very bad, and on May 24 Rawdon wrote as follows to Cornwallis:

> Lieutenant-Colonel Balfour was so good as to meet me at Nelson's. He took this measure that he might represent his circumstances to me. He stated that the revolt was universal, and that, from the little reason to apprehend this serious invasion, the old works of Charleston had been in part levelled, to make way for new ones which were not yet constructed; that its garrison

was inadequate to oppose any force of consequence; and that the defection of the townspeople showed itself in a thousand instances. I agreed with him in the conclusion to be drawn from thence, that any misfortune happening to my corps might entail the loss of the province."

Lee joined Sumter before Augusta on May 21, and on June 5 the garrison was compelled to surrender by the artifice of the wooden towers. On May 22 Greene began the siege of Ninety-Six, and he was joined by Lee and Pickens after the fall of Augusta. The post was held by 550 New York Loyalists.

Meanwhile, on June 3, reinforcements reached Charleston from Ireland. They consisted of the 3rd, 19th, and 30th Regiments, besides some recruits for the Guards. Rawdon decided to march at once to the relief of Ninety-Six, with 1,800 infantry, 200 cavalry, and some Carolina Loyalists. Marion and Sumter failed to delay him. On June 18 Greene assaulted Ninety-Six, but the attack failed, and on the 20th he raised the siege and fell back towards the North.

On the following day Rawdon reached Ninety-Six. Finding that Greene had crossed the Broad River, he decided to evacuate Ninety-Six and concentrate his forces. Ninety-Six was abandoned on July 3, and on the 14th Rawdon had concentrated his forces at Orangeburg. The heat during this retirement had been terrific, and fifty soldiers had died of sunstroke.

The hardships endured by the soldiers in this summer campaign are described by Tarleton in the following words:

During renewed successions of forced marches, under the rage of a burning sun, and in a climate at that season peculiarly inimicable to man, they were frequently, when sinking under the most excessive fatigue, not only destitute of every comfort, but almost of every necessary which seems essential to his (sic) existance. During the greater part of the time they were totally destitute of bread, and the country afforded no vegetables for a substitute. Salt at length failed; and their only resources were water, and the wild cattle which they found in the woods.

On July 20 Rawdon handed over the command to Colonel Stewart, of the 3rd Foot, and marched with 500 men to Charleston. His health had been broken down by the hardships of the campaign, and on arrival at Charleston he embarked for England.

The ship on which he sailed was captured by a French privateer, and Rawdon was taken to Brest as a prisoner of war, but soon afterwards he was exchanged, and he returned to England.

In accordance with the custom of English politicians, the Opposition in Parliament made all the capital it could out of the war, and the army was accused of employing "methods of barbarism." In February, 1782, an attack was made upon Lord Rawdon in the House of Lords. A motion was brought forward to condemn the execution of a certain Isaac Haynes, who was taken in arms after he had given his parole. The motion was defeated, and Rawdon demanded and obtained a public apology from the mover.

In March, 1782, Rawdon was appointed lieutenant-colonel of the 105th Foot, and in November he was promoted colonel and appointed *aide-de-camp* to the king.

Thus the advent of peace in 1783 found Lord Rawdon, at the age of twenty-eight, a colonel and *aide-de-ca*mp to the king. it must be confessed that his subsequent career as a soldier was far from fulfilling the brilliant promise of his youth.

In June, 1793, Rawdon succeeded his father as Earl of Moira. A few months later he was promoted major-general, and in June, 1794, he was despatched from Southampton with 10,000 men to help the Duke of York in Flanders.

The force landed at Ostend, and Moira effected his junction with the Austrian general, Clerfayt, at Alost on July 6, after a dangerous flank march. Clerfayt greeted him with the words: "*Vous, milord, avez su faire l'impossible.*" To deceive the French, and thus render his junction with Clerfayt possible, Moira ordered rations for 25,000 troops to be prepared. The ruse was successful, but the Treasury ordered Moira to pay out of his own pocket for the extra 15,000 rations. The general refused to pay, but after his death the Treasury extorted the money from his widow.

Moira joined the Duke of York on July 8. On the 12th the British were driven back to Malines, and shortly afterwards they retired to Antwerp.

This was Moira's last campaign before he embarked for India as governor-general in April, 1813. Opportunities were plentiful in those stirring times, and a man of his ability and influence could not have failed to obtain employment as a soldier had he desired it, but he preferred to dabble in politics, and to waste his time and his money in the society of the Prince of Wales.

In 1797 he caused great amusement by writing a letter in which he stated that many Members of Parliament had proposed that he should be Prime Minister, and declared that he was ready to form an Administration. On hearing of this, Cornwallis wrote as follows:

> It is surely impossible that Lord Moira's letter can be genuine; if it is, excess of vanity and self-importance must have extinguished every spark of understanding, and I am sure there was a time when he had sense.

In 1804 he married Flora, Countess of Loudoun, and she became the mother of six children.

He was made a Knight of the Garter in 1812. He sailed from Portsmouth on April 14, 1813, reached Calcutta on October 4, and assumed the office of governor-general. He was responsible for the Ghurka and Maratha Wars, and he did not leave India till January 1, 1823.

In February, 1817, he was created Marquess of Hastings, Earl of Rawdon, and Viscount Loudoun, and in the following year he was made a G.C.B. and G.C.H.

Owing to his extravagance, he had to seek employment again after his return from India, and in March, 1824, he was made governor of Malta. He died on November 28, 1826, and was buried in Malta. He left directions that his right hand should be cut off and buried with his wife when she died.

In person he was tall and dark. He was said to be "the ugliest man in England," but his bearing was stately and dignified. His manner was genial, and it was said of him that:

> No man possessed in a higher degree the happy but rare faculty of attracting to him all who came within the sphere of his command.

GENERAL THE MARQUESS OF HASTINGS (LORD RAWDON), K.G., G.C.B., G.C.H.

Ensign, 15th Regiment, August 7, 1771.
Lieutenant, 5th Regiment, October 20, 1773.
Captain, 63rd Regiment, July 12, 1775.
Major, 1778.
Lieutenant-Colonel, June 15, 1778.
Lieutenant-Colonel, 105th Regiment, March 21, 1782.
Colonel and *Aide-de-Camp* to King, November 20, 1782.
Major-General, October 12, 1793.

Lieutenant-General, January 1, 1798.
General, September 25, 1803.

Colonel, 27th Regiment, May 23, 1804.
Master of the Ordnance, February 8, 1806.
Constable of the Tower, March 1, 1806.

5

Simcoe

John Graves Simcoe, the eldest son of Captain John Simcoe of the Navy, was born at Cotterstock, in Northamptonshire on February 25, 1752. Captain John Simcoe, who had been a member of Admiral Byng's court-martial, died before Quebec in 1759, and shortly afterwards his widow moved to Exeter with her two children. Young Simcoe was first sent to a school in Exeter, and in 1766 he went to Eton. In February, 1769, he went to Merton College, Oxford; but he did not remain long at the university, for on April 27, 1770, he was gazetted an ensign in the 35th Foot.

Two years later Ensign Simcoe was appointed adjutant, and he was promoted lieutenant in March, 1774. He did not accompany the regiment to America, but he landed at Boston on the day of Bunker's Hill. He was a distant relation of Admiral Graves, who commanded the fleet at this time, and he persuaded the admiral to ask General Gage to allow him to raise a corps of negroes for service in Rhode Island. Gage replied that the negroes were not sufficiently numerous, and that he had other employment for those at Boston. In December, 1775, Simcoe was promoted captain in the 40th Foot.

Captain Simcoe served through the New York campaign of 1776, in command of the grenadier company of the 40th. During the following winter he came into New York to apply for the command of the Queen's Rangers, which was then vacant, but he did not secure it. Just before embarking for the Chesapeake in the summer of 1777, he asked General Grant to use his influence to get him the command of a provincial corps like the Queen's Rangers. He was wounded at the Battle of Brandy wine on September 11, 1777, and a month later his wishes were fulfilled, for on October 15 he was appointed to the command of the Queen's Rangers, with the temporary rank

JOHN GRAVES SIMCOE

of major. He joined the regiment next day. On the 20th a draft of nearly 100 recruits arrived, and the regiment was organized in eleven companies—Eight battalion companies, a grenadier company, a light company, and a Highland company wearing the national dress and provided with a piper.

The Queen's Rangers were raised by Colonel Rogers in Connecticut and New York. Colonel French and Major Wemyss each held the command for a time, and Major Simcoe was the fourth commanding officer. Like the other provincial corps, the Rangers were recruited from American Loyalists; but they were supposed to have the exclusive right of enlisting "old countrymen," as Europeans were called, and deserters from the rebel army.

At this time the Rangers were an infantry regiment, but Major Simcoe got leave to mount a few of his men, instead of calling on the cavalry to detail dragoons to assist him, and in a short time the Hussars of the Rangers numbered thirty. The infantry wore green coats and waistcoats with white breeches, while the mounted men were clothed entirely in green. Having had one of his men killed by mistake, Simcoe gave them all black hats of a peculiar shape, to distinguish them both from the Royal Army and from the American forces. The Hussars were armed with a sword "and such pistols as could be bought or taken from the enemy." Simcoe wished to add a dagger to their equipment, to encourage the idea of getting to close quarters. A sergeant of the 16th Light Dragoons was attached as an instructor.

Simcoe regarded the weakness of his companies as a positive advantage, for a corps like the Rangers required a large percentage of officers. Many of his men were very imperfectly trained; but "two files in the centre and two on each flank were directed to be composed of trained soldiers, without regard to their size or appearance."

No time was devoted to ceremonial movements. Simcoe describes the training of his men as follows:

A few motions of the manual exercise were sufficient. They were carefully instructed in those of firing, but above all, attention was paid to inculcate the use of the bayonet, and a total reliance on that weapon.

Officers and men were thoroughly trained in the duties of protection, and their commanding officer claimed that "the Queen's Rangers never gave a false alarm, or had a sentinel surprised, during the war."

Simcoe insisted on his officers carefully supervising the interior economy of their companies, and pointed out to them that "regularity in messing and cleanliness in every respect conduced to the health of the soldier." He maintained a strict discipline in the regiment, and sternly repressed all looting; but having "accidentally heard a man say it was not worthwhile to bring in a prisoner, he therefore made it a rule that anyone who took a prisoner, if he publicly declared he had his watch, should keep it; so that no soldier was interested to kill any man."

In November Lieutenant Ross of the 35th was appointed second-in-command of the Queen's Rangers, with the rank of captain-commandant.

Throughout the winter the Queen's Rangers were engaged in protecting the collection of supplies for the army in Philadelphia, and they had many skirmishes with the enemy. Major Simcoe looked forward eagerly to an attack on the American position at Valley Forge. He was well acquainted with the ground, for he had formerly been quartered in the house which was Washington's headquarters.

In March, 1778, the strength of the Rangers was 270 rank and file infantry and thirty Hussars. On the 18th they had a smart skirmish at Quintin's Bridge, and before dawn on the 21st they surprised a party of the enemy at Hancock's House, and despatched them with the bayonet.

As the time drew near for the evacuation of Philadelphia, the Queen's Rangers were sent out to collect horses. A three-pounder was now added to the regiment. At the beginning of June, Simcoe was given the temporary rank of lieutenant-colonel, and antedated so as to make him senior to the other officers commanding provincial corps.

On June 17 the Queen's Rangers crossed the Delaware to Cooper's Ferry. During the retreat from Philadelphia, Simcoe was able to provide guides, for he kept a book "in which was inserted the names of every soldier in his corps, the counties in which they were born, and where they had ever lived, so that he seldom was at a loss for guides in his own corps."

On the evening of June 25 two Americans who were reconnoitring the British camp mistook an officer of the Rangers for one of Lee's legion. The officer introduced Simcoe as Colonel Lee, whereupon the Americans told him all they knew about their own troops, and then added, "I wonder what Clinton is about "

"You shall ask him yourself," said Simcoe, "for we are British."

The army halted on the 27th, and on the 28th the Battle of Monmouth Court House was fought. Early in the day a reconnoitring party appeared near the Cranberry Road, and Simcoe was ordered to try and cut them off. He took with him twenty Hussars, and his grenadier company, which was forty strong. The country was thickly wooded, and he ran into a large party of the Jersey Militia, who had been ordered to attack the baggage. Simcoe at once attacked them and drove them off, but he was severely wounded in the arm, and five of his men were wounded—one mortally.

Simcoe's wound was very painful, and he was obliged to hand over the command of the Rangers to Captain Ross. June 28 was said to be the hottest day known for many years. Clinton reported that sixty of his men died of sunstroke, and it speaks volumes for the discipline and physical fitness of the Rangers that on such a day they "did not have a man missing or any who fell out of the ranks through fatigue." When the retreat was continued at midnight the Queen's Rangers covered the rear.

Lieutenant-Colonel Simcoe resumed command of the Rangers on July 1, on which date they marched to Sandy Hook. He had good reason to be proud of his regiment during this retreat, when the discipline of many corps was seriously impaired. He summed up the matter in the following words:

It is remarkable, and what few other corps in the army could say, that on this march the Queen's Rangers lost no men by desertion.

There was a widespread belief that the British Army was going to evacuate New York and be transferred to the West Indies. Acting on this report, Simcoe sent in an application that the Queen's Rangers and other Loyalists might join the Indians and the troops under Colonel Brown on the upper waters of the Delaware. General Clinton replied that "he much applauded his spirit, but that he would find sufficient employment for him with his army."

Simcoe was ill in New York for several days, but he was able to rejoin his regiment on July 14. Next day the Rangers advanced beyond Kingsbridge, and an amusette with three artillerymen was added to their three-pounder.

At this time Simcoe was the senior commanding officer of provincial corps, but on August 1 Lord Cathcart was given the temporary rank of colonel. Simcoe protested vigorously at being superseded in this manner. Clinton offered to give him the rank of colonel, but this he foolishly declined. A few days later, however, Lord Cathcart was called away on other duties, and Simcoe was left in command of the light troops in advance of Kingsbridge. Besides the Rangers, he had another provincial corps and the cavalry of the British legion under Tarleton, of whom he says "in Lieutenant-Colonel Tarleton he had a colleague full of enterprise and spirit, and anxious for every opportunity of distinguishing himself."

Simcoe and Tarleton had a very narrow escape one day. They were out together, and were riding quite unconsciously into an ambuscade, when for some trivial reason they changed their mind and turned back.

On August 31 the light troops had a smart skirmish with the Indians, in which forty of the latter were killed and wounded. On this occasion Simcoe was wounded for the third time, while Tarleton in striking at an Indian lost his balance and fell from his horse. The British casualties were only one killed and three wounded.

In the autumn Major-General Grant was sent to the West Indies. He told Simcoe that he would ask General Clinton's permission to take the Queen's Rangers with him. This would have insured the regiment being brought on to the British establishment, and so would have given the officers permanent army rank, but Lieutenant-Colonel Simcoe declined the offer as being unfair to his American soldiers.

During the autumn the Rangers had many skirmishes with the enemy, and Simcoe captured a partisan named Thomas by marching fifty miles in a day.

On November 19 the regiment took up its quarters for the winter at Oyster Bay in Long Island, and the post was at once strongly fortified. It was a good station, for the water was excellent and the men got plenty of vegetables. General Clinton authorized Simcoe to increase the number of his Hussars to fifty. Recruits were hard to obtain, for those who joined provincial corps did not receive so large a bounty as those who enlisted for British regiments. To overcome this difficulty Simcoe and his officers subscribed largely to the bounty fund of their regiment, and an advertisement was inserted in Rivington's *Royal Gazette* at New York stating that "All Aspiring Heroes have now the opportunity of distinguishing themselves by joining the Queen's Rangers Hussars," and that every hero will be "mounted on an elegant horse."

The winter was devoted to the thorough training of the men. The infantry were practised in attacking an enemy posted behind fences; they were taught not to fire, but to run up to the fence and then fire at the enemy point-blank. They were also constantly practised in charging. The light infantry were trained to run with the cavalry, holding the manes of the horses; and all the Rangers were instructed in making rafts and improvising methods of crossing streams. An officer of the Rangers, who suggested a plan for burning the whale-boats of the enemy at Norwalk. was at once sent into headquarters; for in the words of their colonel, "the officers of the Queen's Rangers always understood that whatever plans they might offer for the good of the King's service, would be patronized and fairly represented to the commander-in-chief by their lieutenant-colonel that they might reap the fruit of their own exertions."

On May 18, 1779, the Queen's Rangers left Oyster Bay with a strength of 360 rank and file in first-rate condition. They reached King's Bridge on the 27th, and for the next two months they were constantly engaged in skirmishing with the enemy. They received the title of the 1st American Regiment, and on June 23 Simcoe was given the local rank of lieutenant-colonel.

On July 10, while the regiment was on rear guard, three stragglers were captured by the enemy This was the first occasion on which such a thing had happened since Simcoe assumed command in October, 1777.

On August 8 the light troops fell back to the redoubts at King's Bridge, and the Queen's Rangers were allowed to take off their clothes a night for the first time since they left their winter quarters at Oyster Bay. On October 24th regiment embarked, but landed again and marches to Richmond in Staten Island.

Lieutenant-Colonel Simcoe received intelligence that the enemy had fifty flat-boats on carriages at Van Vacter's Bridge on the Rariton, and he determined to destroy them. He embarked at 3 a.m. on October 26, with 80 cavalry and 300 infantry of the Rangers, and landed at Amboy. He told his officers that he meant to burn the boats at Van Vacter's Bridge, and, crossing the Rariton at Hillsborough, to return by Brunswick, and endeavour to entice the militia there into an ambush. Most of the boats had been removed, but he found eighteen at the bridge, and destroyed them. Unfortunately his guide missed the way owing to a house, which marked the place where the track left the main road, having been destroyed. The result was that Simcoe with his cavalry ran into a party of the enemy, and in the skirmish which ensued his horse was killed, and he was stunned by the fall and taken prisoner. His men returned safely to Amboy.

One of the Americans wanted to bayonet Simcoe as he lay senseless, but their leader said:

> Let him alone, the rascal is dead enough.

Simcoe wrote as follows to Sir Henry Clinton:

> My life was preserved by the eagerness with which, as I have been informed, I was plundered when in a state of insensibility, and afterwards by the humanity of a Mr. Morris.

For some days Lieutenant-Colonel Simcoe was a prisoner on parole, and was frequently insulted and threatened by the Americans; but on November 9 he was taken to Burlington and confined in the gaol. A few days later he was moved into the felons' room. He was treated in this outrageous manner by the local authorities, because American prisoners who were not officers were confined in New York.

It is pleasant to record the fact that while Simcoe was still a prisoner at large he received a letter from Colonel Lee offering to lend him any money he might require. "Light Horse Harry" Lee, the father of the illustrious general of the South, played a distinguished part in the War of the Revolution. He and Simcoe thoroughly appreciated each other's soldierly qualities, and he speaks as follows of the affair in which Simcoe was captured:

"This enterprise was considered by both armies among the handsomest exploits of the war. Simcoe executed completely his object, then deemed very important, and traversed the country from Elizabethtown Point to South Amboy, fifty-five miles, in the course of the night and morning passing through a most hostile region of armed citizens; necessarily skirting Brunswick, a military station; proceeding not more than eight or nine miles from the legion of Lee, his last point of danger, and which became increased from the debilitated condition to which his troops were reduced by previous fatigue."

Sir Henry Clinton had officially reported Simcoe's death, whereupon Lord George Germaine wrote as follows:

> The loss of so able and gallant an officer as Colonel Simcoe is much to be lamented; but, I hope, his misfortune will not damp the spirit of the brave Loyalists he so often led with success. His last enterprise was certainly a very bold one; and I should be glad if he had been in a situation to be informed that his spir-

ited conduct was approved by the king.

An exchange was arranged. Lieutenant-Colonel Simcoe was released on December 27, and he rejoined his regiment in their winter-quarters at Richmond in Staten Island on the 31st.

The weather at this time was very severe, and on January 1 it was impossible to cross to Staten Island because of ice, and the troops had to be put on half rations. There were 1,800 soldiers in the island. The cold weather lasted, and soon the ice was strong enough to bear troops. On the 15th, 3,000 Americans marched across to the island. The position of the garrison was precarious, but after a few days the enemy retired, and many deserters joined the Queen's Rangers. Not a man of the Rangers deserted while the enemy were in the island. Apparently after the retirement of the enemy some of the Rangers had begun to undress at night, for on January 25 the colonel notified them that "he expects the order relative to officers and soldiers sleeping in their clothes to be strictly complied with, such recruits excepted whom the officers commanding companies may judge as yet unequal to the duties of the regiment; if any half-bred soldier disobeys this order, the officer or N.C.O. who meets with him will deliver him to the officer on guard to be put on some internal duty."

Simcoe received information that General Washington's headquarters were dangerously exposed, and on the 31st he asked permission to endeavour to surprise and carry off the American commander. His plan was to take eighty men with an officer to every six men besides his staff, and to attack Washington's quarters at daybreak.

Captain Beckwith, *aide-de-camp* to General Knyphausen, who commanded at New York, had suggested a similar plan, and the Hussars of the Rangers were placed at his disposal for the attempt.

On February 22 the ice broke up and became impassable, so the troops on Staten Island were permitted to undress at night.

Lieutenant-Colonel Simcoe had applied for permission for the Rangers to join General Clinton in the South. He asked Cornwallis to support his application; but meanwhile he requested that boats sufficient to carry 60 cavalry and 300 infantry might be placed at his disposal, so that he might harass the enemy in the Jerseys. He was particularly anxious to surprise Lee's legion at Burlington.

On March 23 orders were received for the infantry of the Rangers to embark for Charleston. They embarked on April 4, 400 rank and file in first-rate condition, and reached Charleston on the 21st.

The Rangers were posted four miles from Charleston, to cover the rear of the troops engaged in the siege, between the Ashley and Cooper Rivers. Simcoe had brought with him one sergeant and nine Hussars, these he quickly mounted and used for patrolling. Two guns were attached to the regiment, and Simcoe arranged for fire-rafts to illuminate the river should the garrison of Charleston attempt to escape by water.

On May 12 Charleston surrendered, and next day Sir Henry Clinton wrote to Lord George Germaine about the colonel of the Rangers as follows:

> Lieutenant-Colonel Simcoe has been at the head of a battalion since October, 1777; and since that time has been the perpetual advance of the army. The history of the corps under his command is a series of gallant, skilful, and successful enterprises against the enemy; without a single reverse. The Queen's Rangers have killed or taken twice their own numbers. Colonel Simcoe himself has been thrice wounded; and I do not scruple to assert that his successes have been no less the fruit of the most extensive knowledge of his profession which study and the experience within his reach could give him, than of the most watchful attention and shining courage.

On May 31 the Rangers embarked once again, and on June 21 they landed on Staten Island and marched to Richmond.

Next day the regiment crossed to Elizabethtown Point, and it took part in the action at Springfield on the 23rd. In this little expedition the Rangers lost 2 men killed and 1 officer and 9 men wounded. The regiment was suffering much from the effects of the short campaign in the South, and at the end of the month Lieutenant-Colonel Simcoe had to go into hospital at New York.

On July 19 Lieutenant-Colonel Simcoe resumed command of the Rangers, and the regiment was moved to Long Island. Towards the end of the month Clinton embarked 6,000 troops to attack the French in Rhode Island. Simcoe sent in an application that the Queen's Rangers might take part in the proposed expedition, and he received the following reply from Major André: "The general assures you that the Rangers shall be pitted against a French regiment the first time he can procure a meeting."

The scheme came to nothing, and the troops were all landed again on July 31. On August 23 the Rangers arrived once more at Oyster

Bay, and two days later the commander-in-chief added two troops to the Hussars and made Simcoe a lieutenant-colonel of cavalry.

Simcoe had been informed of the negotiations which were in progress between Major André and General Benedict Arnold, and in the forthcoming operations he was to have commanded the cavalry. He pointed out that his Hussars were not trained in the regular duties of cavalry, and requested that forty men of the 17th Light Dragoons might be attached to the Rangers. He proposed to add to them forty of his best men and to keep these eighty as a formed body to deal with the enemy's cavalry, while the rest of his Hussars performed the duties of light troops. The unfortunate André was captured on September 23 and hanged on October 2. Simcoe was much distressed at his death, and the Queen's Rangers wore black and white feathers in their hats as a sign of mourning.

On October 8 the Rangers were moved across to Staten Island. At this time the Pennsylvania Loyalists petitioned that Lieutenant-Colonel Simcoe might be sent to the Delaware with 1,000 men, and promised to join him in large numbers. Naturally enough Simcoe was very anxious to undertake the enterprise, and begged that he might be allowed to occupy Billing's Port below Philadelphia; but Sir Henry Clinton, who had a healthy distrust of plans which depended for their success on the co-operation of the inhabitants, wisely refused to sanction the project.

The Queen's Rangers embarked at New York on December 11, and sailed ten days later under Brigadier-General Benedict Arnold for Virginia. It seems strange that Sir Henry Clinton should entrust a traitor with an independent command of this sort, but there appears to be small doubt that he did not altogether trust him, and that he gave a dormant commission to Colonels Dundas and Simcoe to supersede and arrest Arnold if necessary. The commander-in-chief wrote to Lord George Germaine as follows: "This detachment is under the command of General Arnold, with whom I have thought it right to send Colonels Dundas and Simcoe, as being officers of experience and much in my confidence."

Meanwhile Lieutenant Cooke of the 17th Light Dragoons was ordered to raise another troop of Hussars at New York for the Rangers.

Part of the force reached the Chesapeake on December 30, and Arnold at once pushed up the river. On the evening of January 3, 1780, Lieutenant-Colonel Simcoe with 130 of the Rangers and the flank companies of the 80th seized a battery at Hood's Point. Next day the force landed at Westover, only 800 strong, for some of the vessels had not arrived. Arnold decided to march at once on Richmond, which he occupied after a skirmish on January 5. Simcoe was despatched with the Rangers and the flank comanies of the 80th to destroy a foundry at Westham six miles away. The troops left Richmond on the morning of the 6th, and were back at Westover on the 7th. The Rangers were much exhausted by their long marches, and nine men were left behind during this retirement. The Hussars were very badly mounted, for they had had a rough voyage from New York and "the horse vessels were very bad. infamously provided, and totally unfit for service, in consequence of which forty horses had to be thrown overboard."

Simcoe with forty Hussars patrolled towards Long Bridge, and skirmished with the American militia. On January 10 the troops embarked at Westover and dropped down the river. Four days later they landed at Harding's Ferry, and marching by Smithfield reached Portsmouth on the 19th. Arnold at once began to fortify the place.

The Queen's Rangers were sent on January 29 to fortify a post at Great Bridge, but they returned to Portsmouth on February 6. Lieutenant-Colonel Simcoe was always thinking of means to increase the mobility of his regiment, and we learn that at this time he "had converted the bodies of his waggons into small pontoons, capable of holding six men, as boats, and well adapted to form bridges over the small creeks in the country, through which, if it had become necessary to quit Portsmouth, the retreat might have been made to North Carolina."

On March 18 Lafayette appeared before Portsmouth, and Arnold ordered all the male inhabitants to work on the lines or else to leave the town. On the 27th Major-General Phillips arrived, bringing with him 2,600 fresh troops, and assumed the command. As a young artillery officer Phillips had distinguished himself at Minden, and in the advance from the North in 1777 it was he who suggested dragging guns to the summit of Mount Defiance, which resulted in the capture of Ticonderoga.

Simcoe applied for some gunners to be attached to the Rangers to man his guns, but Phillips would only sanction a few men being lent for a short time as instructors. Simcoe then pointed out that the regiment was now weak in numbers, and that his men were more useful with muskets, and on April 20 he handed into store the three-pounder and the *amusette*.

Major-General Phillips issued orders that officers commanding units or detachments were to keep regular journals, which they were to hand in when called upon. Leaving a garrison at Portsmouth, he embarked the bulk of his force, and landed it at City Point on April 24. He occupied Petersburg on the 25th after a smart skirmish with the enemy, and he destroyed two 20-gun vessels, a 16-gun brig, and several small armed craft. The troops halted for three days at Petersburg, and then marched to Bermuda Hundreds, where they embarked on May 2.

Phillips was now very ill, and Arnold assumed the command. On the 7th the troops again advanced to Petersburg to effect a junction with Cornwallis, who was advancing from the South. Simcoe was careful to run no risk of falling in with Tarleton's cavalry by night for fear of accidents. He got into touch with Cornwallis on the 14th, and with Tarleton on the following day. On the 20th the whole force was assembled at Petersburg under Cornwallis. The army passed the River James on the 24th, and on the 29th Captain Cooke's troop from New York joined the Rangers near Newcastle, but they brought with them neither arms nor equipment.

Two of the Rangers were convicted of robbery and rape, and duly hanged. This sort of thing was by no means unusual in some provincial corps, but it was the first instance in the Queen's Rangers since Simcoe assumed the command. The regiment was much reduced in strength, and there were scarcely more than 200 infantry and 100 Hussars fit for duty—fifty of the men were barefooted.

Lieutenant-Colonel Simcoe was now despatched with the Rangers and the 71st Highlanders (200 strong) on a raid to Point of Fork. On his way he found Steuben with a force of militia on the far side of the River Fluvana. The Americans retired, and Simcoe constructed a raft which would carry 130 men. He reached Point of Fork on June 7th, and destroyed 2,500 stand of arms besides large quantities of powder and stores, and he carried off some guns which were afterwards mounted on the defences of Yorktown. Two days later he destroyed 150 barrels of powder and much tobacco.

The army reached Richmond on June 16. In order to deceive the enemy who were close behind, Simcoe one evening paid a large sum of money to a man whom he knew to be a rebel. He told the fellow to visit Lafayette's camp and return to him next morning at 7 a.m. Simcoe sent off his infantry and baggage at 2 a.m., and followed with the cavalry at 3 a.m. At 4 a.m. "Mad Antony" Wayne, profiting by the lesson which he had learnt at Paoli, charged into the deserted camping-ground.

On June 26 Simcoe had a smart little action at Spencer's Ordinary, near Williamsburg. The enemy were 1,200 strong, while the Rangers and the *Jagers* were only 400, but Simcoe repulsed the Americans, and at the close of the action Tarleton arrived with the cavalry of the Legion. Simcoe regarded this action as "the climax of a campaign of five years, and the result of true discipline acquired in that space by unremitted diligence, toil, and danger." The Rangers had 10 men killed, 2 officers and 21 men wounded, while the *Jagers* lost 1 killed and 3 wounded. The Americans lost 2 officers and 7 men killed, 4 officers and 10 men wounded, and 32 of them were taken prisoners. Two days later Cornwallis paid a visit to Yorktown escorted by Simcoe and his cavalry.

Early in July the army crossed the James River and proceeded to Portsmouth. The Queen's Rangers embarked at Portsmouth on July 20, and landed at Yorktown on August 2.

On the 12th the Rangers crossed the river to Gloucester to protect the foraging parties on that side. When the French fleet appeared at the end of August, Cornwallis asked Simcoe whether he thought he could make his escape with the cavalry, and the latter replied: "Without the smallest doubt."

Lieutenant-Colonel Simcoe was very ill from the effects of fatigue and exhaustion. On October 2 the Legion was brought across to Gloucester, and Tarleton assumed the command on that side. On the 3rd Tarleton had a skirmish with the French, and a report spread that he had been defeated; thereupon Simcoe had himself carried from his bed to a horse, and went to the redoubt, which was manned by his men.

When Cornwallis opened negotiations for the surrender of his army on October 17, Simcoe pointed out that the Queen's Rangers consisted of Loyalists and of deserters from the American Army, and asked permission to cross the Chesapeake, land in Maryland, and endeavour to reach New York. Cornwallis replied that all must share alike. When the Capitulation was signed the strength of the Queen's Rangers was 39 officers, 3 quarter-masters, 2 surgeons, and 277 men. By the terms of the surrender the sloop *Bonetta* was sent to New York with Clinton's despatches. The doctors declared that a sea-voyage was the only chance of saving Simcoe's life, so he was sent on the *Bonetta* together with as many American deserters serving in the Rangers and other corps as could be stowed on board. These were to remain at New York until exchanged.

Simcoe's health was quite broken down, so he returned to England, where he soon recovered. He was promoted brevet lieutenant-colonel on December 19, 1781. The officers of the Rangers were naturally very anxious that their regiment should be taken on the British establishment, which would give them army rank. This application was warmly supported by Sir Henry Clinton, not only as an act of justice to the officers, "but in justice to his country, that in case of future war it might not be deprived of the services of such a number of excellent officers." The regiment was taken on the British establishment on December 25, 1782, and Simcoe was gazetted its lieutenant-colonel.

On December 30 he married Elizabeth, daughter of Colonel Gwillim, of Old Court, Hereford, and on January 14, 1783, he was released from his parole. It was not fated that the Queen's Rangers should take the field again. Peace had been made with the United States, and in 1783 the regiment was disbanded and the officers were placed on half-pay. Many of the officers and most of the men settled in Nova Scotia.

Lieutenant-Colonel Simcoe passed the next eight years quietly in England. In 1787 his *Journal of the Operations of the Queen's Rangers* was printed privately at Exeter. In 1789 he applied for permission to raise a corps to consist of one troop of Hussars, four troops of Dragoons, eight battalion companies, two grenadier companies, and two light companies. In the British Museum may be seen the copy of the *Journal* which Simcoe sent to the King. It contains a copy of his petition and an autograph letter dated London, March 15, 1789, which begins as follows:

> The journal of the operations of the Queen's Rangers, which is accompanied by this letter, was principally composed to confirm, in some measure, by actual experience what otherwise might appear to be too theoretical.

The application was not successful. In 1790 he was returned as Member of Parliament for St. Maw's in Cornwall, and he was promoted colonel in November. In 1791 he was appointed the first lieutenant-governor of Upper Canada, and he was gazetted colonel of the Queen's Rangers on September 1.

In Canada he found full scope for his energy, and proved himself an excellent administrator. He remained in the country for five years.

He selected Newark (Niagara) as the first capital of his province, but in 1793 he moved the seat of government to Toronto. During his tour of office he founded the town of London and named the River Thames. He did everything possible to increase the population, and allotted lands to half-pay officers, American Loyalists, and soldiers who had served for some years in Canada. He did not conceal his dislike of the United States.

The Duke de la Rochefoucault, in his *Travels in North America in 1795*, speaks thus of the lieutenant-governor:

> But for this inveterate hatred against the United States, which he too loudly professes, and which carries him too far, General Simcoe appears in the most advantageous light. He is just, active, enlightened, brave, frank, and possesses the conidence of the country, of the troops, and of all those who join him in the administration of public affairs. To these he attends with the closest application; he preserves all the old friends of the king, and neglects no means to procure him new ones. He unites, in my judgement, all the qualities which his station requires to maintain the important possession of Canada, if it be possible that England can long retain it.

He was promoted major-general in October, 1794, and he returned to England in 1796.

In 1793 a small British force was despatched to St. Domingo. Reinforcements were sent from time to time, but affairs in the island had been going from bad to worse. The mortality and sickness among the troops were appalling, and there was a serious rising of the negroes and mulattos. To meet this state of affairs corps of militia both black and white were raised, and officered by French colonists and *émigrés*. The one idea of these gentry was to make money out of the British government, so peculation and corruption were rife.

On November 30, 1796, Simcoe was appointed to command the troops in St. Domingo, with the local rank of lieutenant-general. he was instructed to protect those who had called the British to their assistance, but to do so by means of local troops, as the Government would send no more British troops to the island. Finally, and most important of all, the cost of defending St. Domingo must not exceed £300,000 a year. In 1796 the cost had exceeded £2,000,000, and £700,000 was spent in January, 1797!

Simcoe wished to occupy the island of Tortuga, and, using it as a base, to land wherever he liked and strike at the enemy. He reached Mole St. Nicolas on February 20, 1797, and at once saw that the extreme weakness of his British regiments and the worthlessness of his foreign troops rendered vigorous action impossible. He immediately set to work to suppress abuses, whereupon two *émigré* officers evacuated the posts which had been entrusted to their charge. A few reinforcements reached the island in April, and Simcoe drove back the negro leader Toussaint from his positions near Port-au-Prince, but he was obliged to suspend his operations to relieve the post of Irois.

In June an expedition against the enemy failed owing to the incompetence of a brigadier. Simcoe was disgusted at the weakness of his force, which reduced him to impotence, and wrote:

> Not a day has passed since my arrival in which a reinforcement of two thousand troops or six thousand new troops would not have insured the conquest of French St. Domingo.

In the middle of June, Simcoe reported that he did not think it possible both to hold the island and to reduce the expenditure to the extent required; and in July he returned to England, as had been arranged.

He was appointed colonel of the 22nd Foot in June, 1798. On January 1, 1801, Simcoe was promoted lieutenant-general, and in the course of the year he was appointed to the command of the troops at Plymouth. In 1806 he was appointed commander-in-chief in India, but he was ordered first of all to join Lord St. Vincent in the Tagus. He was taken very ill at sea, and obliged to return home. He landed at Torbay, and died shortly afterwards at Exeter on October 26.

There is a monument by Flaxman in Exeter Cathedral, but, as is only fitting, the grandest memorial to Simcoe is in Ontario, where a lake, a county, and a town, all bear his name.

In considering the services rendered by Simcoe during the war in America, it is inevitable that one should compare him with Tarleton. Tarleton certainly had the more brilliant record, but then he had far greater opportunities. As commander of the cavalry he was able to distinguish himself at the battles of Camden and Guildford, and when acting independently he achieved the most brilliant results at Biggin's Bridge, the Waxhaws, and in dealing with Sumter at Fishing Creek.

Simcoe did not have anything like the same chances. Until quite near the end of the war the Hussars of the Rangers were very few in numbers; and, though the infantry of the Rangers took a small part in the operations which resulted in the fall of Charleston, Monmouth Court House was the only important battle at which the regiment was present after Simcoe assumed the command on October 15, 1777. On the other hand, the Rangers were constantly engaged in desultory operations near New York, which gave no opportunity for brilliant feats of arms on a large scale.

We have already seen what Sir Henry Clinton thought of the colonel of the Rangers, but probably there is no praise which Simcoe himself would have valued so highly as that of his gallant opponent Colonel Lee, who said of him:

> He was enterprising, resolute, and persevering; weighing well his project before entered upon, and promptly seizing every advantage which offered in the course of execution.

Lastly, Simcoe established and maintained in the Rangers a state of discipline which would have done credit to regular troops, while Tarleton's men remained badly disciplined ruffians to the end of the war.

When Yorktown fell in October, 1781, Simcoe was twenty-nine years old and Tarleton twenty-seven. The difference in character between the two men is shown by their subsequent careers. While Tarleton merely led a life of pleasure, Simcoe did good service in Canada and St. Domingo, and was appointed commander-in-chief in India. He was a man of much more solid character than Tarleton. As a commanding officer he always saw that his subordinates got the credit for any good work they did, and in his *Journal* he delighted to record the gallant deeds of officers and men of the Queen's Rangers.

The energy with which he took steps to settle old soldiers and Loyalists near the American frontier in Upper Canada bore good fruit when the war with the United States broke out in 1812. One cannot help feeling that, had he lived, he would have rejoiced in seeing the result of his labours.

LIEUTENANT-GENERAL JOHN GRAVES SIMCOE.

Ensign, 35th Foot, April 27, 1770.
Adjutant, 35th Foot, March 27, 1772, till December 26, 1775.
Lieutenant, 35th Foot, March 12, 1774.
Captain, 40th Foot, December 27, 1775.
Major, August 4, 1780.
Lieutenant-Colonel, December 19, 1781.

Lieutenant-Colonel, 1st American Regiment (Queen's Rangers), December 25, 1782.
Colonel, November 18, 1790.
Major-General, October 3, 1794.
Lieutenant-General, January 1, 1801.

Colonel, Queen's Rangers, September 1, 1791.
Colonel, 22nd Foot, June 18, 1798.

Temporary Major, October 15, 1777.
Temporary Lieu tenant-Colonel, October 15, 1777.
Local Lieutenant-Colonel, June 23, 1779.
Local Lieutenant-General, November 30, 1796.

6

Tarleton

Banastre Tarleton, the third son of John Tarleton, was born at Liverpool on August 21, 1754. His father was mayor of Liverpool in 1764.

Young Tarleton was educated at Oxford and entered one of the Inns of Court, but in April, 1775, he was gazetted cornet in the 1st Dragoon Guards. He was with the regiment only a few months, for he volunteered for service in North America, and sailed on December 26.

Tarleton arrived at Cape Fear early in May, 1776, and took part in Clinton's abortive expedition to Charleston in the following month. In Howe's New York campaign he served with the cavalry under Sir William Erskine, being present at White-plains on October 28, and at the capture of Fort Washington and Fort Lee. On December 13 he was in command of the advanced guard of the patrol which captured General Lee, and in January, 1777, he took part in the operations near Princetown and Trenton under Cornwallis.

Tarleton had already distinguished himself, and he was now appointed a captain in Harcourt's Horse, and also brigade-major. In July he sailed with Sir William Howe's force to Elk Head, and he was present at the Battles of Brandy-wine and Germantown.

On January 8, 1778, Tarleton was gazetted captain in the 79th Foot, but he remained doing duty with the cavalry. He was never conspicuous for unassuming modesty, and at the famous *meschianza* in April, he appeared as one of the knights bearing on his banner the motto: "*Swift, vigilant, and bold.*"

He remained at Philadelphia till it was evacuated, was present at the battle of Monmouth Court House in June, and was with the rear-guard during the retirement to New York. At this time he was not

BANASTRE TARLETON

quite twenty-four years old, and he had had three years' service.

Among the provincial corps raised while the army was at Philadelphia was one called the Caledonian Volunteers. The Caledonian Volunteers were originally light infantry, but early in 1778 the corps was reconstituted by Sir William Cathcart as a mixed force of cavalry and infantry, and named "The British Legion." A troop of the 17th Light Dragoons was attached to the Legion as a training establishment.

On August 1, 1778, Tarleton succeeded to the command of the Legion, with the temporary rank of lieutenant-colonel. During the autumn the Legion was engaged in frequent skirmishes with the enemy in front of King's Bridge, and the new commanding officer devoted himself to the thorough training of his officers and men in all the duties of light troops. Tarleton was promoted brevet-major in August, 1779.

The British Legion formed part of the force which sailed from New York on December 26, 1779, under Sir William Clinton. The weather was very rough, and the vessels did not reach Tybee, in Georgia, till the end of January. All the cavalry horses had died at sea. The infantry of the Legion was landed at Tybee and formed part of the force which was to march from that place to Charleston under Brigadier-General Patterson. Tarleton was sent with his cavalry to Port Royal Island, where he managed to procure horses in sufficient numbers but of very inferior quality. He then joined Patterson on his march to Charleston.

The siege now commenced, and it was not long before Tarleton had a chance of distinguishing himself. The American General, Huger, had taken up his position with three regiments of cavalry and some militia at Biggin's Bridge on the Cooper River, about thirty miles from Charleston, to keep open the communications between Charleston and the North. Clinton despatched Lieutenant-Colonel Webster with 1,400 men to deal with this force.

Webster with the 33rd and 64th Regiments reached Goose Creek on April 12, and sent Tarleton forward the same evening with the Legion and Ferguson's Riflemen in the hope of surprising the enemy. From a captured negro Tarleton learnt that the American cavalry were on the near side of the river, while the militia were at a meeting-house on the other side near Biggin's Bridge. The surprise was complete, and Tarleton rushed the enemy's camp at 3 a.m. on April 13. The British casualties only amounted to 1 officer and 2 men wounded, with 5 horses killed and wounded, while Tarleton captured 100 of the enemy besides 50 loaded waggons, and—most valuable of all—400 horses with which he could remount his men.

Tarleton summed up the action in the following words:

> This signal instance of military advantage may be partly attributed to the judgement and address with which this expedition was planned and executed, and partly to the injudicious conduct of the American commander, who, besides making a false disposition of his corps, by placing his cavalry in front of the bridge during the night and his infantry in the rear, neglected sending patrols in front of his *vedettes*; which omission equally enabled the British to make a surprise, and prevented the Americans recovering from the confusion attending an unexpected attack.

Unfortunately, after this action some of Tarleton's men broke into a house, and were guilty of excesses.

Webster arrived during the day with the infantry, and at once sent on Tarleton to seize all boats and take possession of Bonneau's Ferry.

On April 25 Lord Cornwallis, who was in command of the troops to the East of the Cooper River, placed Tarleton in charge of the country between the Cooper and the Wando, and at the same time added the following caution:

> I must recommend it to you in the strongest manner to use your utmost endeavours to prevent the troops under your command from committing irregularities.

At 3 p.m. on May 25 Tarleton, with 150 of his dragoons, surprised and routed at Lenew's Ferry some American cavalry who were marching down the right bank of the Santee River. The Americans lost 7 officers, and 36 men killed and wounded, and 7 officers and 60 men taken prisoners together with all their horses, and 18 prisoner; whom they had taken were recaptured.

Tarleton only lost 2 men and 4 horses in the action, but more than 20 horses died on the return march to Huger's Bridge that evening.

Charleston surrendered on May 12, and up to this date the casualties of Tarleton's Legion had only amounted to 5 men killed and 9 wounded.

Clinton now decided to return to New York with a portion of his army; but he arranged for one column to move up the Savannah River, a second to go to Ninety-Six, and a third under Cornwallis to strike at Colonel Buford who was retiring to North Carolina.

Cornwallis left Huger's Bridge on May 18 with 2,500 men, and reached Nelson's Ferry on the 26th. The heat proved very trying to the troops.

On May 27 Cornwallis directed Tarleton to push on after Buford. To use his own words:

> Lieutenant-Colonel Tarleton on this occasion was desired to consult his own judgement, as to the distance of the pursuit or the mode of attack. To defeat Colonel Buford and to take his cannon would, undoubtedly in the present state of the Carolinas, have considerable effect; but the practicability of the design appeared so doubtful, and the distance of the enemy so great, that the attempt could only be guided by discretional powers, and not by any antecedent commands.

Tarleton's force consisted of 40 of the 17th Light Dragoons, 130 dragoons of the Legion, 100 mounted infantry of the Legion, and a three-pounder.

Many of the horses were knocked up by the heat, but Tarleton requisitioned others, and reached Camden on the 28th.

There he learnt that Colonel Buford had left Rugeley's Mills two days before, on the way to Charlotte in North Carolina. Tarleton left Camden at 2 a.m. on the 29th, reached Rugeley's Mills at dawn, and learnt that the enemy were still twenty miles ahead. In spite of fatigue, and the exhaustion of the horses, Tarleton pushed on. He sent forward an officer to magnify his numbers and demand the surrender of the enemy; but Colonel Buford was not to be delayed in that manner. Many of Tarleton's men dropped behind, and the three-pounder could not keep up, but at 3 p.m. he overtook the enemy on the borders of North and South Carolina, after a march of 105 miles in fifty-four hours.

Colonel Buford had 380 Continental infantry, a detachment of cavalry, and two six-pounders. He posted his infantry in line in an open wood, keeping a small reserve in hand, and he ordered his guns and waggons to continue the march escorted by his cavalry. Tarleton describes his own dispositions as follows:

> Lieutenant-Colonel Tarleton made his arrangement for the attack with all possible expedition. He confided his right wing, which was composed of sixty dragoons, and nearly as many mounted infantry, to Major Cochrane, desiring him to dis-

mount the latter, to gall the enemy's flank before he moved against their front with his cavalry. Captains Corbet and Kinlock were directed, with the 17th Dragoons and part of the Legion, to charge the centre of the Americans; whilst Lieutenant Colonel Tarleton, with thirty chosen horse and some infantry, assaulted their right flank and reserve. This particular situation the commanding-officer selected for himself that he might observe the effect of the other attacks.

He also arranged that as the stragglers arrived they should form up on an eminence near the road as a rallying-point.

The action now commenced. The Americans who held their fire till the British were within ten paces, were completely broken by the charge. Tarleton's horse was shot under him. A report went round that their leader was killed, and the men of the Legion determined to avenge his fall.

The Americans had 14 officers and 99 men killed, and 8 officers and 142 men wounded and left on parole; while 3 officers and 50 men were captured together with two six-pounders. The losses of the British in this remarkable action of the Waxhaven were only 2 officers, 3 men, and 11 horses killed 1 officer, 11 men, and 19 horses wounded.

Tarleton points out that this crushing defeat was due to the mistakes made by the America commander. If Buford had formed his waggons into a *laager*, the British could have accomplished nothing. It was also a serious mistake to hold their fire till the dragoons were within ten paces for it was impossible to stop the rush of the horses.

On the evening of May 30 Tarleton moved off again, and he rejoined Cornwallis at Camden a few days later.

An advance into North Carolina was out of the question for the next three months, so in the middle of June Cornwallis went to Charleston to arrange about the administration of the province, leaving Rawdon in command of the troops upcountry.

Rawdon distributed the troops widely, both to protect the Loyalists and to enable the soldiers to live on the country. Camden was strongly held, and there were detachments at Georgetown, Cheraws, Rocky Mount, Ninety-Six, and Augusta. The troop of 17th Dragoons was ordered back to New York, and the work of keeping up communication between all the different detachments devolved on the dragoons of the Legion—much to the disgust of their commanding officer, who wrote:

This service injured them infinitely more than all the preceding moves and actions of the campaign, and though hitherto successful against their enemies in the field, they were nearly destroyed in detail by the patrols and detachments required of them during the intense heat of the season.

By the end of June a force of 2,000 men under Baron de Kalb had entered North Carolina, and this advance led to much unrest in South Carolina. A partisan named Sumter, who had fought under Braddock, was especially active; he attacked Rocky Mount on July 30, and Hanging Rock on August 6.

On July 24 General Gates assumed the command of the American troops. He advanced at once and on July 10 he reached Lynch's Creek—thirteen miles north of Camden—where he found Lord Rawdon in position.

In the meantime Lieutenant-Colonel Tarleton had had an attack of fever, in consequence of which he was sent down to Charleston. On recovering from his illness he received orders to rejoin Rawdon with as many of his dragoons as he could collect. On August 6 he crossed the Santee at Lenew's Ferry with thirty dragoons and forty mounted militia. He made a rapid march up the left bank of the Black River, and, by passing his men off as American troops, not only secured much valuable information, but arrived at Lynch's Creek on the 10th, bringing with him as prisoners a party of militia, who had accompanied him for the purpose of falling upon the rear of Rawdon's posts.

On the 13th Rawdon fell back to Camden, where he was joined by four companies of light infantry from Ninety-Six. Cornwallis arrived from Charleston on that night, and next day, at Tarleton's request, he ordered all the horses with the army to be assembled, and handed over all the best to the British Legion.

On the 15th Tarleton captured three Americans about ten miles north of Camden, and learnt from them that Gates had ordered his troops to march that night to attack the British at dawn next day. Tarleton at once mounted his prisoners behind three dragoons and brought them to Cornwallis. The earl decided to advance and attack the Americans, and by a strange coincidence both armies moved off at 10 p.m.

When the Battle of Camden began at dawn on August 16 the Legion cavalry (10 officers and 171 men) were posted in column to the right of the road near the first battalion of the 71st Highlanders, who were in reserve.

The British right under Webster soon broke the American militia who were opposed to them. They then wheeled in on the left flank of the troops who were engaged with Rawdon.

The cavalry were now launched against the flank and rear of the Americans, and the retreat soon became a rout. Tarleton pursued the enemy relentlessly for twenty-two miles to Hanging Rock, and captured many prisoners, twenty ammunition waggons and 150 store waggons. The cavalry rejoined Cornwallis the same afternoon at Rugeley's Mills.

On the 14th Gates had sent 100 regulars, 300 militia, and two guns to Sumter, who was ordered to harass the British line of communications.

Sumter now had 800 men under his command, and on the 15th he captured two convoys, together with their escorts of 100 British regulars and 150 militia.

At dawn on the 17th Cornwallis detached Tarleton with the cavalry of the Legion and the light infantry to pursue Sumter, who was certain to be falling back.

Tarleton's force consisted of 350 men and one three-pounder. He advanced up the left bank of the Wateree, picked up twenty prisoners, and learnt that Sumter was retiring up the right bank. At dusk he reached Rocky Mount and saw the enemy's fires about a mile away. He at once secured all boats, and forbade any lights or fires.

At dawn Sumter's rear-guard was seen to leave Rocky Mount, and resume the march up the right bank of the Wateree. The British crossed the river, and continued the pursuit, but at noon they had reached Fishing Creek without coming up with the enemy. The men were now very exhausted by the heat and the length of their march, so Tarleton decided to continue the pursuit with 10 dragoons and sixty light infantry, while the remainder of his little force, with the gun, took up a position near Fishing Creek to form a rallying point. The pursuit was continued for five miles further, and then two of the enemy's *vedettes* fired on the advanced guard. They were at once cut down. A sergeant signalled back from a neighbouring rise, and Tarleton on joining him saw the American camp just beyond the crest of the hill. The enemy, thinking the shots were fired by their own men at cattle, were taking their ease.

Tarleton immediately formed his cavalry and infantry into one line, charged into the camp, and secured the arms of the Americans before they could fall in. A few shots were fired from the waggons, but in a few minutes 150 of the Americans were killed and wounded, and 200 more taken besides two guns, 1,000 stands of arms, and all their waggons.

The captured British regulars and loyal militia were set free, but the necessity of guarding so many prisoners and the exhaustion of the troops prevented along pursuit. Sumter himself escaped without his coat, hat, or boots.

Tarleton rejoined Cornwallis at Camden on the 21st. His losses in this brilliant little action only amounted to 1 officer and 8 men killed, 6 men wounded, and 20 horses killed and wounded.

For the next three weeks there was a lull in the operations, while supplies and reinforcements were hurried forward from Charleston; but the advance into North Carolina was begun in the middle of September. Cornwallis with the main body moved up the left bank of the Wateree, while Tarleton moved up the right bank with the British Legion and the light infantry. Ferguson with the militia was farther to the west. Tarleton now had another violent attack of fever, so he was not with his regiment at the skirmish outside Charlotte. The country round Charlotte was the most disaffected district in the Carolinas, and during the halt here the British foraging parties were constantly harassed and messengers shot down.

An American attack on Augusta was repulsed, but on October 7 Major Ferguson was defeated and killed at King's Mountain. Rumours of this action reached Charlotte, but nothing was known for certain, so on the 10th Cornwallis ordered Tarleton to march to the assistance of Ferguson with the Legion, the light infantry, and a three-pounder. Tarleton soon learnt that the bad news about Ferguson was true, and he at once informed Cornwallis. He was just planning another blow at Sumter when he was recalled to the Catawba.

In consequence of Ferguson's defeat, Cornwallis decided to give up his plan of invading North Carolina, and to fall back. The British troops left Charlotte on the evening of the 14th, abandoning twenty waggons laden with supplies, and the baggage of Tarleton's force. The army halted for two days owing to the illness of Cornwallis, but Rawdon assumed the command and brought the troops back to Winnsboro. By the end of the month Cornwallis had recovered.

The action at King's Mountain had greatly encouraged the disaffected in South Carolina, and Marion, "the Swamp Fox," was especially active in the neighbourhood of the lower Pedee. Cornwallis sent Tarleton with the Legion and the light infantry to quell these disturbances.

Tarleton left Camden on November 4, and by skilfully concealing his numbers, on the 10th he nearly entrapped Marion, who was advancing with 500 militia to attack him. The Americans were within two miles of the British position before they learnt their mistake, but they managed to make their escape; and Tarleton was now hurriedly recalled to deal with Sumter.

The operations against Marion were by no means fruitless, and on December 3 Cornwallis wrote as follows to Clinton:

I therefore sent Tarleton, who pursued Marion for several days, obliged his corps to take to the swamps, and by convincing the inhabitants that there was a power superior to Marion, who could likewise reward and punish, so far checked the insurrection, that the greatest part of them have not dared to appear in arms against us since his expedition.

On November 11 Cornwallis ended a letter to Tarleton with the following words:

I wish you would get three legions, and divide yourself into three parts. We can do no good without you. I trust to your coming immediately, unless you see something more materially pressing.

Tarleton at once returned through Camden to Winnsboro, and thence to Brierley's Ferry on the Broad River, where he found the 71st Highlanders and a detachment of eighty mounted infantry of the 63rd Regiment. Cornwallis now ordered him to take the mounted infantry of the 63rd as well as his Legion and the light infantry, and deal with Sumter, who was approaching Ninety-Six.

Tarleton concealed the green uniform of his dragoons, so that the enemy should not know of his return from the east. He crossed the Broad River after dark on the evening of the 18th, and obtained information that Sumter was advancing with 1,000 men to attack a small post fifteen miles from Ninety-Six.

Tarleton made a long march on the 19th, and encamped for the night near the Ennoree. All had gone well. The enemy had not discovered him, and one more march would have enabled him to surprise the Americans, had not a man of the 63rd deserted that night and warned Sumter of his peril.

Tarleton resumed his march at dawn on the 20th, and at 10 a.m. he encountered and cut up a detachment of the enemy at a ford on the Ennoree Sumter with his main body had passed the river two hours before. The British troops pushed on till 4 p.m., when it became clear that it was impossible for the infantry to overtake the enemy before they passed the Tiger River.

Tarleton now left the light infantry and the infantry of the Legion to follow with the three pounder, while he hastened on with the 170 dragoons of the Legion and the 80 mounted infantry of the 63rd. He overtook the enemy at 5 p.m. at Blackstocks House. Sumter had posted his men in some log-houses, so Tarleton dismounted the 63rd and part of his dragoons and intended to wait for his infantry.

Sumter determined to seize his opportunity, and attacked the 63rd, who were hard pressed, but Tarleton charged with his dragoons and saved the situation. Darkness now came on, and the Americans retired across the river and dispersed In this action the British lost 6 officers and 45 men killed and wounded. Fifty of the Americans were captured and Sumter was severely wounded, but the numbers of their casualties are very uncertain.

Tarleton pursued the remnant of Sumter's force for three days, and then fell back quietly to Brierley's Ford on the Broad River.

Cornwallis was preparing to invade North Carolina again when he had received the reinforcements which were marching up from Charleston under General Leslie; but before the end of December he received information that General Greene, who now commanded the American troop in the South, had divided his small force of regular; giving his light infantry and the cavalry under Colonel Washington to Morgan with orders for him to threaten Ninety-Six, while he himself, with the remainder of his men, joined Caswell on the Pedee to threaten Camden.

On January 1 Cornwallis ordered Tarleton to cross the Broad River with the Legion and the light infantry (550 strong), the 71st Fraser's Highlanders (200 strong), and two three-pounders, and to fall on Morgan.

Finding that Morgan was still very distant, Tarleton halted to await his baggage, and suggested that Cornwallis should move up the Broad River to King's Mountain, and that he himself should endeavour to drive Morgan in that direction. Cornwallis approved of this plan.

Tarleton's baggage arrived escorted by 50 men of the 17th Light Dragoons, and 200 men of the 7th Regiment (mostly recruits) who were intended to be left in garrison at Ninety-Six, but Tarleton was authorized to take them with him. Tarleton crossed the Ennoree and Tiger Rivers on the 14th, and learned that Morgan was holding the fords on the Pacolet. The British troops crossed the Pacolet on the morning of the 16th, and the Americans retreated.

The pursuit was resumed at 3 a.m. on the 17th, but the country was much intersected by creeks and ravines, so the advance was very slow.

At dawn Tarleton pushed his cavalry to the front, and it was not long before they came upon the enemy, who were drawn up in an open wood, at a place called the Cowpens.

The Americans were fresh, and had had breakfast, but Tarleton decided to attack at once, for in the rear of the enemy flowed the Broad River, and behind that Cornwallis was to have been at King's Mountain to cut off their retreat. The numbers on both sides were about equal.

Morgan drew up his infantry in three lines. In front he posted 150 picked marksmen, with orders to fire at the officers and then retire. Behind these were 300 militia, with orders to fire two rounds at killing range and then retire, while on an eminence in the rear were posted his regular infantry, 430 strong. Hidden behind this rise in the ground were the cavalry (125 strong), under Colonel Washington.

Tarleton kept the 71st Highlanders and 200 of his cavalry in reserve, while the rest of his infantry advanced in line to the attack, with a party of fifty Dragoons covering each flank.

The American militia fell back after delivering a destructive fire, and Tarleton now brought up the 71st Highlanders against the right flank of the American regulars. Morgan ordered one battalion to change front to oppose the 71st. This was badly done, and the whole line retired. The British, thinking the victory won, pressed on in great disorder. Meanwhile the American militia, after passing round the rear of their regulars, reappeared on the American right flank. Morgan ordered his line to halt and turn about, and they delivered a deadly fire at thirty paces. The effect was overwhelming. The British wavered, and then broke and fled, but the gunners defended their guns till they were all shot down. Tarleton made vain efforts to rally the infantry, and the dragoons of the Legion galloped from the field. The detachment of the 17th Light Dragoons alone stood firm, and Tarleton, placing himself at the head of a party of fourteen officers and forty men, charged and drove back the American cavalry, and endeavoured to cover the retreat.

This action at the Cowpens was a crushing disaster, and Tarleton's column was practically annihilated. The casualties of the British amounted to 100 killed, 239 wounded, and 400 taken prisoners; 39 officers were killed and wounded, the two guns were lost, and also the colours of the 7th Regiment.

The American losses were only twelve killed and sixty wounded.

Morgan retreated at once across the Broad River, taking with him the captured guns, the prisoners, and 800 stands of arms.

As he fell back Tarleton learned that Cornwallis, far from being at King's Mountain to co-operate with him, was twenty-five miles away at Turkey Creek.

Tarleton cannot be blamed for attacking Morgan when he found him with a deep river in his rear especially as he had reason to believe that Cornwallis was waiting to intercept the enemy. Morgan made the most judicious use of his militia, but Tarleton had no reason to suppose that his men would give way in panic as they did.

Two hundred dragoons of the Legion fled to the camp of Cornwallis, and a few more stragglers rejoined Tarleton next day. Leslie's reinforcements arrived on the 18th, and on the 19th Cornwallis began his advance. Greene hoped to oppose him on the Catawba. On the 25th Cornwallis halted at Ransour's Mills, and destroyed all surplus stores and baggage.

Tarleton asked Cornwallis to hold an inquiry into the action at the Cowpens, but on the 30th the earl wrote as follows:

You have forfeited no part of my esteem as an officer by the unfortunate event of the action of the 17th. The means you used to bring the enemy into action were able and masterly, and must ever do you honour. Your disposition was unexceptionable; the total misbehaviour of the troops could alone have deprived you of the glory, which was so justly your due.

The British forced the passage of the Catawba before dawn on February 1. Tarleton learnt that some of the American militia were to assemble at Tarrant's Tavern at 2 p.m. that day, and he deter-mined to attack them. He bade his men "Remember the Cowpens," and then gave the order to charge. The enemy, who were about 400 strong, were broken instantly, some fifty were killed, wounded, or captured, and the remainder were dispersed.

The Americans continued their retreat, and crossed the Dan into

Virginia on February 14. Cornwallis then fell back, by easy marches, to Hillsborough. On the 22nd Greene recrossed the Dan, and four days later Cornwallis left Hillsborough. The British troops marched west and crossed the Haw.

Cornwallis had 2,250 troops present and fit for duty; and Greene, who was camped at Guildford, twelve miles away, was reported to have over 7,000 men. The British troops were badly in need of supplies of all kinds. To remain where they were was impossible. The only alternatives were to attack the enemy or to retreat, and Cornwallis chose the former. Before dawn on March 15 he sent off his baggage and sick under an escort of 350 men, and he advanced with 1,900 soldiers to attack the enemy at Guildford.

The advance guard, under Tarleton, encountered Lee's Dragoons about four miles south of Guild-ford, and brushed them aside; and about noon the British troops arrived near the American position.

Greene actually had 4,500 men under arms, of which 1,700 were regulars and 2,800 militia, and in drawing up his men he copied Morgan's dispositions at the Cowpens. In front he placed 1,600 North Carolina Militia, with a body of riflemen on either flank. Three hundred yards behind these were the Virginia Militia, 1,200 strong; and 600 yards in rear, again, were the regulars.

Leslie's brigade formed the British right, and Webster's the left. The two battalions of Guards were kept in reserve, and also the cavalry. Tarleton received instructions "not to charge without positive orders, except to protect any of the corps from the most evident danger of being defeated."

About 1.30 p.m. the British infantry advanced to the attack, and the North Carolina Militia, after losing only eleven men killed and wounded, fled from the field. The riflemen on their flanks offered so stout a resistance that a battalion on either flank had to wheel outwards to deal with them, and the two battalions of Guards were brought up to fill the gaps.

Tarleton's cavalry were thus the only reserve.

The Virginia Militia, who formed the second line, behaved well; but Webster quickly overcame the brigade that opposed him. He then attacked the American regulars, who formed the third line, but he was repulsed. A second attack was delivered by the Guards, but they too were driven back. Leslie had by this time overcome the militia who were opposing him, and Greene decided to retire,

Cornwallis sent one squadron of cavalry to hang on the rear of the

Americans, and ordered Tarleton with the remainder to charge a body of the enemy who were still offering resistance on the British right. The charge was successful, and the engagement now came to an end, for the British were in no condition to pursue.

The behaviour of the British troops was magnificent, but the best comment on the folly of Cornwallis in fighting this battle may be found in the following passage in Greene's despatch to Washington dated March 16:

> I took the resolution of attacking the enemy without loss of time, and made the necessary disposition accordingly, being persuaded that if we were successful, it would prove ruinous to the enemy, and, if otherwise, it would only prove a partial evil to us.

Tarleton fully agreed with Greene, and wrote:

> A defeat of the British would have been attended with the total destruction of Earl Cornwallis's infantry, while a victory at this juncture could produce no very definite consequences against the Americans.

The British lost 93 killed, and 439 wounded, including 28 officers killed and wounded. Lieutenant-Colonel Tarleton was severely wounded in the right hand. According to General Greene's returns, the Americans lost 11 officers and 68 men killed, 28 officers and 158 men wounded. In addition 161 regulars and 25 officers and 860 men of the militia were missing two days after the battle. Their four guns were captured.

Greene took up another position behind the Haw only 10 miles from Guildford. Cornwallis halted for two days, and on the 18th— leaving 70 of his most severely wounded under a flag of truce—he commenced his retreat to Cross Creek, and thence to Wilmington, which he reached on April 7.

Information was now received that Greene was marching on South Carolina. When Tarleton was consulted as to the practicability of marching from Wilmington to Virginia or to South Carolina, he replied that he thought both quite feasible, and offered, if the rest of the force went by sea to Charleston, to march to South Carolina with his Dragoons and one company of mounted infantry.

Cornwallis recklessly determined to leave South Carolina to its fate, and to march into Virginia, where there were 4,200 British troops under Phillips and Benedict Arnold. He left Wilmington on April 28 with 1,600 men, and his advanced guard was commanded by Lieutenant-Colonel Tarleton.

At the beginning of May Tarleton pushed on with 180 of his dragoons and two companies of mounted infantry—the light companies of the 82nd and of a North Carolina regiment. He crossed the River Tarr, and hurried on to Halifax, where he had a skirmish with a party of militia. Some of the enemy took up a position on the other side of the Roanoke, and Tarleton asked that the light company of the Guards might be mounted and sent forward to him, but Cornwallis replied that he had no horses for them.

As soon as Cornwallis reached Halifax, he directed Tarleton to push on with his cavalry and mounted infantry. They had not gone more than four miles when Cornwallis overtook them, and ordered Tarleton to form up his dragoons in single rank, as some outrages had been committed the previous evening. A sergeant and private of the dragoons were at once identified, tried for murder and rape, and summarily executed at Halifax.

On May 15 Tarleton got into touch with Simcoe, who commanded the light troops of Arnold's force. General Phillips had died a week before.

Arnold's force was at Petersburg, and on May 20 Cornwallis arrived there with his troops and assumed the command. A few days later he learnt of Rawdon's victory at Hobkirk's Hill, and on the 23rd he received a reinforcement of 1,500 men consisting of two British and two German battalions, which brought his strength up to 7,300 men.

Tarleton was now sent out to get information about the enemy, and near Warwick Court-house he fell in with 400 American militia. Owing to heavy rain the enemy could not use their muskets, so Tarleton routed them with but few casualties to the dragoons and brought in 50 prisoners.

On the 26th Cornwallis crossed the James River at Westover, and advanced to the North Anna River, where he halted.

On June 4 Tarleton set out with 180 dragoons, and 70 mounted infantry of the 23rd Regiment, to surprise the Assembly of Virginia at Charlotteville. He covered the 70 miles in 24 hours, and galloped into the town. A few of the enemy were killed, and seven members of the Assembly were captured. Tarleton destroyed 400 barrels of powder and 1,000 firelocks, and he was joined by 20 of Burgoyne's soldiers, who were working near the town.

He left Charlotteville the same afternoon on his return march.

Cornwallis now marched west, and on the 7th he camped near Point of Fork, and ordered Tarleton to provide horses to mount the 76th Regiment.

The army left Point of Fork on the 14th, and arrived at Williamsburg on the 25th. Tarleton and Simcoe had covered this retirement, and they had a smart skirmish with the enemy outside Williamsburg on the morning of the 26th.

At Williamsburg Cornwallis received instructions from Sir Henry Clinton to send at once to New York as many troops as he could spare. On July 4 the army marched to a position opposite James Island, and Tarleton, who was ordered to cover the right flank and rear with his dragoons and the two companies of mounted infantry, took advantage of heavy rain to drive in the picquets of Lafayette's force.

The operation of passing the waggons and stores across to the island required three days. On the 6th the cavalry reported that the enemy were advancing. Tarleton sent a negro and a dragoon to go to the enemy in the guise of deserters, and inform them that the British had crossed the James River with the exception of a rear-guard consisting of the Legion and a detachment of infantry. Lafayette fell into the trap, and that afternoon he crossed a swamp with 2,500 men and attacked the British outposts.

Cornwallis now fell upon the Americans, and drove them back across the swamp in confusion, with the loss of their guns, but the darkness prevented a pursuit. In this affair the British casualties amounted to only 5 officers wounded and 70 men killed and wounded, while the Americans lost 26 killed, 99 wounded, and 12 missing.

At dawn next morning Tarleton started in pursuit with 200 dragoons and 80 mounted infantry. He found the enemy, halted only six miles away, overcome by fatigue, but Cornwallis neglected to avail himself of the opportunity. The British troops crossed the James River on the 7th.

On the 9th Cornwallis despatched Tarleton with his dragoons and 80 mounted infantry on a long raid to destroy stores between the James and the Dan. Tarleton learnt that Greene was besieging Ninety-Six; but the raid was a failure, for the stores destroyed were not sufficient to compensate for the losses sustained.

The dragoons and mounted infantry after covering more than 400 miles in fifteen days rejoined the army at Suffolk. Cornwallis now marched to Portsmouth, and to quote Tarleton's own words:

> . . . . . at this period the British Legion received new clothing and appointments, which were soon properly fitted, and, for the first time, that corps was properly equipped.

At Portsmouth Cornwallis received permission to retain all his troops, but Clinton directed him to fortify a post at Old Point Comfort for the protection of the fleet. The engineer and naval officers all reported adversely on Old Point Comfort, so Cornwallis decided to fortify Yorktown and Gloucester instead.

Portsmouth was evacuated, and the army was assembled at Yorktown and Gloucester by August 22. The dragoons were taken across to Hampton in small vessels, and the horses were thrown out of the ships in deep water and swam ashore without loss.

The York River is not more than a mile wide between Yorktown and Gloucester. While the infantry were occupied in throwing up works for the defence of these positions, Simcoe on the Gloucester side and Tarleton in front of Yorktown were collecting forage and driving in cattle.

Tarleton made several expeditions to Williamsburg, and on one occasion he broke up a party of 300 militia twelve miles beyond that place.

On the 30th the French fleet under De Grasse appeared off the mouth of the Chesapeake, and the situation was completely changed. The French troops brought from the West Indies were at once landed, and on September 3 they joined Lafayette at Green Springs.

Lafayette now advanced to Williamsburg with 4,000 men. Cornwallis received information that Washington was hastening south with a large force of Americans and French, and as he had 6,000 troops available he made up his mind to attack Lafayette before Washington arrived.

Tarleton carried out a successful reconnaissance of the enemy's position, but at this juncture, on receiving a letter from Clinton saying that he would do all he could to assist him, Cornwallis gave up his idea of falling upon Lafayette and so threw away another golden opportunity.

On September 14 Washington reached Williamsburg, and by the 26th the French and American forces were concentrated there under his command. On the 28th the allies approached Yorktown.

Tarleton formed up his three squadrons of dragoons in front of the

British position, but he never got a favourable opportunity of striking, and at sunset the cavalry retired inside the position.

On the 29th nothing of note occurred till the evening, when Cornwallis abandoned his outer position without a blow, and fell back on his inner line of work. The allies were now able to commence their siege works, and on the evening of October 2 Cornwallis sent Tarleton's dragoons and mounted infantry across to Gloucester.

On the 3rd a foraging party went out some three miles from Gloucester to bring in Indian corn. The waggons were loaded and retired with their infantry escort, while Tarleton covered the movement with his cavalry. A French force of cavalry and infantry now advanced. Tarleton hid his cavalry in a wood to lie in wait, while he went with a small party to reconnoitre the enemy. A skirmish ensued, and the horse of one of the dragoons of the Legion being wounded with a lance, plunged and knocked over Tarleton's charger. The cavalry in the wood a mile away, seeing their leader's fall, at once galloped to his rescue, but arrived in such disorder that they could not drive back the French cavalry.

Tarleton, who had secured another horse, at once ordered a retreat, checked the enemy by posting forty of his mounted infantry in a thicket, and reformed his dragoons. Thereupon the French cavalry took shelter behind their infantry. In this skirmish the British lost 1 officer and 11 men killed and wounded, and the French 2 officers and 14 men.

On the 4th the French effectually blockaded Gloucester, but they did not undertake siege operations on this side.

On the night of the 6th the allies began their first parallel 600 yards from Yorktown, and Cornwallis was in vain urged to evacuate the place, cross the river, and break out through Gloucester.

On the night of the 11th the enemy began their second parallel. To replace his casualties Cornwallis recalled some of his infantry from Gloucester, and left Tarleton in command at the latter place.

On the evening of the 14th the allies captured two redoubts, A sortie before dawn on the 16th failed to improve matters. The situation was now desperate. At last Cornwallis decided to break out from Gloucester, and he sent orders to Tarleton to make all preparations.

Three trips would have been sufficient to take the troops across the river. The first contingent arrived in safety before midnight, but then a squall came on and interrupted the operations. When the wind dropped Cornwallis decided to bring back the first contingent, and it returned soon after daybreak with but little loss from the enemy's batteries.

All was now over. Before noon on the 17th Earl Cornwallis wrote to General Washington to propose a cessation of hostilities, and the capitulation of Yorktown was signed two days later.

During the siege the British had lost 156 officers and men killed, and 326 wounded. Cornwallis surrendered with 400 officers and 6,600 men exclusive of the hospital staff and non-combatants. Of this number 2,089 were sick. The allies also captured 144 guns, 24 colours, 4 frigates, and 30 transports, besides large quantities of ammunition and stores. The officers were allowed to retain their swords, and those not required to remain with the men were to have the option of returning to England on parole.

The allies had lost 75 killed and 199 wounded, and it is interesting to note that two-thirds of the casualties were sustained by the French. It would seem that even in their crowning victory the Americans were well content to let others bear the brunt of the fighting.

The strength of the British Legion on October 19, 1781, was 24 officers, 1 surgeon, 17 sergeants, 7 trumpeters, and 192 rank and file.

Lieutenant-Colonel Tarleton returned to England on parole early in 1782. He was only twenty-seven years of age, but unfortunately he never had another chance of distinguishing himself in the field. Under Cornwallis he had undoubtedly acted up to his motto, and proved himself "*swift, vigilant, and bold.*" He had owed his marvellous success chiefly to the secrecy and rapidity of his movements, and to the thorough training of his officers and men, but to the end his dragoons were very prone to commit excesses, and he never managed to enforce discipline as successfully as Simcoe.

On his arrival in England, Tarleton found himself a man of note. His portrait was painted by Reynolds and Gainsborough. He was a noted raconteur, and he, like Rawdon, was received into the circle of the Prince of Wales.

In December, 1782, he was gazetted lieutenant-colonel of an American regiment of Light Dragoons, but in the following October he was placed on half-pay.

In 1787 he published his *History of the Campaigns of 1780 and 1781, in the Southern Provinces of North America.* Apart from its interest as a narrative of events by one who played a prominent part in them, this book is valuable because at the end of each chapter it contains the official despatches, returns, and letters, which refer to the operations described.

Tarleton now devoted himself to a life of pleasure and to politics. He failed to get into Parliament in 1784, but in 1790 he was elected at the head of the poll for Liverpool, and he sat from 1790 till 1806, and again after a short break from 1807 till 1812.

He was promoted colonel in November, 1790, and major-general in October, 1794. In 1798 he was sent out to Portugal, but he was re-called at his own request a few months later, and on December 17 he married Susan, the natural daughter of the fourth Duke of Ancaster.

On January 1, 1801, Tarleton was promoted lieutenant-general, and in September, 1803, he was appointed to the Command of the Cork District. From Ireland he was transferred to the Severn district, which he commanded for six years. He was appointed governor of Berwick in 1808, and promoted General in January, 1812.

General Tarleton was created a baronet on November 6, 1815, and a G.C.B. in May, 1820. He died at Leintwardine, in Staffordshire, on January 25, 1833.

GENERAL SIR BANASTRE TARLETON, G.C.B.

Cornet, 1st Dragoon Guards, April 20, 1775.
Captain, 79th Foot, January 8, 1778.
Major, August 11, 1779.
Lieutenant-Colonel, June 15, 1781.
Lieutenant-Colonel, American Regiment of Light Dragoons, December 25, 1782 (half-pay, October 24, 1783-1788).
Colonel, November 18, 1790.
Major-General, October 3, 1794.
Lieutenant-General, January 1, 1801.
General, January 1, 1812.

Temporary Lieutenant-Colonel, August 1, 1778.

Colonel, Durham Fencible Cavalry, May 11, 1799.
Colonel, 22nd Light Dragoons, January 8, 1801.
Colonel, 21st Light Dragoons, April 29, 1802.
Colonel, 8th Light Dragoons, January 15, 1818.

Governor of Berwick, February 23, 1808.

Baronet, November 6, 1815.
G.C.B., May 20, 1820.

7

Ferguson

Patrick Ferguson, the second son of James Ferguson, of Pitfour, in Aberdeenshire, was born in the year 1744. His mother was Anne Murray, a daughter of Lord Elibank, and so General James Murray, of St. Foy and Minorca fame, was his uncle. General Murray was left in command of Quebec, after the death of Wolfe, and in a letter from that city, dated October 11, 1759, he wrote:

> I left orders to send Petty Ferguson to the academy at Wolich.
> I hope it was done. I mean to push him in my own profession.
> I am sure if I live I shall have it in my power; and if I die it will
> not be the worse for him that I had the care of him.

The boy had been sent to a military academy in accordance with his uncle's directions, and on July 12, 1759, he was gazetted as an ensign in the 2nd Royal North British Dragoons (now the Scots Greys). He joined the regiment in Germany soon after the Battle of Minden, so it is probable that he was present at the Battle of Warburg in June, 1760, and also at an action at Zierenberg two months later, in which the North British Dragoons greatly distinguished themselves.

On one occasion during this campaign he and another young officer were riding some way ahead of the army, and they were chased back by a party of the enemy's Hussars. In jumping a ditch, young Ferguson dropped one of his pistols; he at once recrossed the ditch in face of the enemy and picked up his pistol before continuing his retreat. The Hussars, thinking some supports which they could not see must be at hand, stopped their pursuit. Before the campaign of 1760 came to an end young Ferguson fell ill, and, after spending some time in hospital, he was invalided home, much to his annoyance. He wrote as follows:

Patrick Ferguson

I am now entirely recovered, and might serve the next campaign with ease, had not the fears of my parents prompted them to apply for an order for my joining the light troop; by which means I am deprived for these many years to come of the only chance of getting a little insight into my profession.

He took no further part in the war, and remained at home until 1768.

Nothing of much note occurred during these years except that, while on a visit to Paris, he fought a duel with a French officer, who spoke disparagingly of the British Army. Ferguson managed to disarm his opponent, who was a noted swordsman.

In September, 1768, Ferguson purchased his company in the 70th Foot, which was stationed in what the Army List of the time called "The Charibbee Islands." Captain Ferguson joined the regiment in Tobago, and remained in the West Indies till 1774, when he returned to England. He devoted much time to the improvement of fire-arms, and actually invented a breech-loading rifle. The weapon weighed 7½ pounds, and was 50 inches in length. It was provided with a movable backsight for ranges from 100 to 500 yards, and the breach was closed by a vertical screw plug. For use with this weapon he devised a sword-bayonet 25 inches long.

Captain Ferguson gave a demonstration of the capabilities of his rifle, and the Annual Register of June, 1776, contains the following passage:

Some experiments were tried at Woolwich before Lord Viscount Townshend, Lord Amherst, Generals Hervey and Desaguiliers, and a number of other officers, with a rifle gun upon a new construction by Captain Ferguson of the 70th Regiment, when that gentleman, under the disadvantages of a heavy rain and a high wind, performed the following four things, none of which had ever before been accomplished with any other small arms: First, he fired during four or five minutes at a target, at 200 yards distance, at the rate of four shots each minute; second, he fired six shots in one minute; third, he fired four times per minute, advancing at the same time at the rate of four miles in the hour; fourth, he poured a bottle of water into the pan and barrel of the piece when loaded, so as to wet every grain of the powder, and in less than half-a-minute fired with her as well as ever without extracting the ball. He also hit the bull's-eye at 100 yards, lying with his back on the ground; and, notwithstanding the unequalness of the wind and wetness of the weather, he only missed the target three times during the whole course of the experiments. The captain has since taken out a patent for the said improvements.

The king wished to see the new rifle, so Captain Ferguson was ordered to Windsor, and some of the Guards were armed with the new weapon to give a demonstration. The men were nervous in the presence of the king and shot badly. Ferguson remarked: "They would not be so embarrassed in the presence of your Majesty's enemies." He then took a rifle, and, "of nine shots which he fired at the distance of 100 yards, put five balls into the bull's-eye of the target, and four within as many inches of it. Three of these shots were fired as he lay on his back, the other six standing erect. Being asked how often he could load and fire in a minute, he said seven times; but added pleasantly that he could not undertake in that time to knock down above five of His Majesty's enemies."

Ferguson's patent "for various improvements upon firearms, whereby they are loaded with more ease, safety, and expedition, fire with more certainty, and possess other advantages," was dated March 17, 1776.

Captain Ferguson now volunteered for service in America, and special instructions were sent to the commander-in-chief to select picked men from various regiments to be armed with Ferguson's rifle and placed under his command. This appears to have annoyed Sir William Howe, who, being himself the chief authority at that time on light infantry, seems not to have liked receiving instructions of this sort.

However, the rifle corps was duly formed, and it was not long before it had an opportunity to distinguish itself in Pennsylvania. Ferguson's riflemen formed part of the force which landed at Elk Head on August 25, 1777, and they covered the advance of Knyphausen's Division at the Battle of Brandy wine on September 11. The value of a breech-loader was very apparent that day. Ferguson's men could load and fire without exposing themselves, and had only two men wounded (of whom the commanding officer was one), while the Rangers, who were fighting by their side, had seventeen men killed. Captain Ferguson was severely wounded, his right elbow being shattered by a bullet. He was disabled for some months, and never recovered the use of his right arm, so that he had to use both sword and pen with his left hand. Hence it came about that in Carolina he was known among the Americans as "the one-armed devil." Shortly before Ferguson was hit an incident occurred which he described as follows in a letter:

We had not lain long when a rebel officer, remarkable by a Hussar dress, passed towards our army, within a hundred yards of my right flank, not perceiving us. He was followed by another dressed in dark green or blue, mounted on a bay horse, with a remarkable large cocked hat. I ordered three good shots to steal near to them and fire at them; but the idea disgusted me. I recalled the order. The Hussar, in returning, made a circuit, but the other passed again within a hundred yards of us, upon which I advanced from the wood towards him.

On my calling, he stopped; but, after looking at me, proceeded. I again drew his attention, and made signs to him to stop, but he slowly continued his way. As I was within that distance at which, in the quickest firing, I could have lodged half-a-dozen of balls in or about him before he was out of my reach—I had only to determine; but it was not pleasant to fire at the back of an unoffending individual, who was acquitting himself very coolly of his duty; so I let him alone.

The day after I had been telling this story to some wounded officers who lay in the same room with me, when one of our surgeons, who had been dressing the wounded rebel officers, came in and told us they had been informing him that General Washington was all the morning with the light troops, and only attended by a French officer in a Hussar dress, he himself dressed and mounted in every point as above described. I am not sorry that I did not know at the time who it was. Farther this deponent sayeth not, as his bones were broke a few minutes after.

A few days after the battle, Ferguson received the following letter, but when the Brandywine Despatches appeared in the *Gazette* he found that neither he nor his riflemen were mentioned, so he sent a copy of the letter to the Secretary of State.

Headquarters,
September 12, 1777.

Sir,
The commander-in-chief has received from Lieutenant-General Knyphausen the most honourable report of your gallant and

spirited behaviour in the engagement of the 11th, on which His Excellency has commanded me to express his acknowledgements to you, and to acquaint you, sir, that he shall, with great satisfaction, adopt any plan that can be effected to put you in a situation of remaining with the army under his command. For the present, he has thought proper to incorporate the rifle corps into the light companies of the respective regiments. I am very happy to be even the channel of so honourable a testimony of your spirited conduct, and of that of your late corps.

And I am, sir, with perfect esteem and regard.

Your most obedient, humble Servant,

(Signed)   J. Paterson, adjutant-general.

Ferguson was present when Philadelphia was evacuated the following year, and he took part in the Battle of Monmouth Court House on June 28, 1778. Three months later he had an opportunity of displaying his capacity in a most marked manner. It is interesting to note that here, as on the fatal day of King's Mountain, Ferguson showed that though he was the inventor of a rifle, he was fully alive to the value of the bayonet.

He was placed in command of 300 British soldiers and 100 provincials. The little force left New York on September 30, but did not reach Little Egg Harbour, its destination, till October 5. In the meantime the Americans had managed to get several of their privateers away; but the rest were destroyed by H.M.S. *Zebra*, while the soldiers landed and burnt the store-houses.

A deserter now brought news that an American corps, known as "Pulaski's Legion," was billeted, without any military precautions, only twelve miles away, and that Pulaski had neglected to hold a bridge over a creek in his front. Ferguson determined to surprise the enemy, and he accomplished his object with the most conspicuous success. The following is an extract from his report to Sir Henry Clinton dated October 15, 1778, from Little Egg Harbour:

Accordingly, at eleven last night, 250 men were embarked, and, after rowing twelve miles, landed at four this morning within a mile of the defile, which we happily secured, and leaving fifty men for its defence, pushed forward upon the infantry of this legion, cantoned in three different houses, who are almost entirely cut to pieces. We numbered among their dead about fifty, and several officers, among whom, we learn, are a lieutenant-colonel, a captain, and an adjutant. It being a night attack, little quarter could of course be given, so that there are only five prisoners.

As a rebel, Colonel Proctor, was within two miles, with a corps of artillery, two brass twelve-pounders, one three-pounder, and the militia of the country, I thought it hazardous, with 200 men, without artillery or support, to attempt anything farther, particularly after Admiral Gambier's letter. The rebels attempted to harass us in our retreat, but with great modesty, so that we returned at our leisure, and re-embarked in security.

The captain who has come over to us is a Frenchman named Bromville. He and the other deserters inform us that Mr. Polaski has in public orders lately directed no quarter to be given; and it was therefore with particular satisfaction that the detachment marched against a man capable of issuing an order so unworthy of a gentleman and a soldier. It is but justice to inform you, sir, that the officers and men, both British and provincials, on this occasion behaved in a manner to do themselves honour.

  I have the honour to be, etc.,

   (Signed)   Pat. Ferguson, Capt. 70th. Regt.

P.S.—The despatch vessel not having got to sea last night, I am enabled to inform you that our yesterday's loss consists of two men of the 5th, and one of the provincials missing, and two of the 5th slightly wounded. Ensign Campbell of the 2nd Jersey Volunteers has received a stab through the thigh.

We had an opportunity of destroying part of the baggage and equipage of Polaski's legion by burning their quarters; but as the houses belonged to some inoffensive Quakers, who, I am afraid, may have sufficiently suffered already in the confusion of a night's scramble, I know, sir, you will think with us, that the injury to be thereby done to the enemy would not have compensated for the sufferings of these innocent people.

Ferguson took part in Clinton's operations which led to the capture of Stony Point in May, 1779. The Americans, under "Mad Antony" Wayne, recaptured the place on July 17th, but evacuated it next day, after removing the guns and damaging the works. On July 19th the British troops reoccupied Stony Point, and Ferguson was placed in command of the post. He devoted himself to strengthening the place, and looked forward eagerly to the opportunity of testing his arrangements. It was a great disappointment to him when he received orders to evacuate the place and retire with his garrison to New York. One of his letters contains the following passage:

> Never did a fond mother leave her favourite child with more regret than I did that place.

Ferguson was promoted major in the 71st (Fraser's) Highlanders on October 26, 1779.

He was now given the temporary rank of lieutenant-colonel, and placed in command of a corps called "The American Volunteers," which was formed of 300 Loyalists from New York and New Jersey. The corps was armed with Ferguson's rifles and was sometimes known as "Ferguson's Sharpshooters."

The American Volunteers formed part of the force of 7,600 men, which sailed from New York on December 26, under Clinton, for the capture of Charleston; the transports reached Tybee, in Georgia, towards the end of January, 1780. The main body of the expedition sailed again for Charleston, but a small force under Brigadier-General Patterson marched to Charleston from Tybee. Patterson used the American Volunteers and the infantry of Tarleton's Legion under Major Cochrane to cover his advance. Both Ferguson and Cochrane heard that there was an American force on a certain plantation, and each determined to surprise the enemy. Ferguson arrived first, and, finding the place deserted, decided to remain there for the night. Cochrane arrived later, and at once attacked with the bayonet, and Ferguson received a severe wound in his left arm before the mistake was discovered. Ferguson praised the man who had bayoneted him, gave him a piece of money, and remarked:

> We should have known our friends sooner from their mode of attack.

This wound, owing to the bad climate, gave much trouble, and for some time Lieutenant-Colonel Ferguson had to ride between two men, and could only hold the reins in his mouth; but he recovered sufficiently to bear a distinguished part in the siege of Charleston at the head of his regiment.

The American Volunteers were largely employed during the siege in scouring the country and driving off parties of the enemy who approached to harass the besiegers. On one occasion Ferguson captured a convoy of forty waggons.

On April 14 Ferguson's American Volunteers and Tarleton's Legion fell upon the American cavalry, under Huger, at Biggin's Bridge, thirty miles north of Charleston, and captured 400 horses. Several of Tarleton's men then broke into a house and molested some ladies. They were apprehended, and Ferguson wished to execute them on the spot, but he was overruled.

The diary of Lieutenant Allaire (an officer of the American Volunteers) records that on May 2 Ferguson "marched down to Mount Pleasant, and stormed and took possession of a little redoubt, located partly on the main, and partly on the bridge that leads to Fort Moultrie."

After the fall of Charleston on May 12, Sir Henry Clinton returned to New York, leaving Cornwallis to complete the work in the south. There were considerable numbers of Loyalists, mostly of Highland descent, in the Carolinas, and, before his departure, Clinton had selected Ferguson to organize and command the militia of those provinces. The Loyalists came to join him in considerable numbers, till at one time he had 2,000 of them (besides his small corps of American Volunteers, which was now reduced to about 100 men), but their numbers were constantly fluctuating.

Ferguson's duties were extensive and peculiar; besides training the militia, he was responsible for maintaining order generally, and he was even authorized to marry people. Cornwallis, in referring to Ferguson, wrote of "the home duty as being more that of a Justice of Peace than of a soldier."

For the next three months Ferguson was busily engaged in clearing the country of the enemy. His assistant-adjutant-general, Captain Chesney, writes:

Our next route was down towards the Fishdam Ford on Broad River, where there was a fight (August 12) near the mouth of Brown's Creek, with Neil's militia, where we made many prisoners.

The numbers of Ferguson's militia now fell off considerably, but on August 16 came the victory of Camden, and Ferguson was summoned to headquarters by Cornwallis.

Allaire notes in his diary on September 1:

Major Ferguson joined us again from Camden with the disagreeable news that we were to be separated from the army and act on the frontiers with the militia.

Cornwallis now set out for Charlotte, in North Carolina; Tarleton moved up the left bank of the Wateree with his Legion; while Ferguson, with the militia, moved on the extreme left.

It is strange that Cornwallis should have exposed the militia in this manner. They had proved themselves untrustworthy on several occasions, and on August 20 Cornwallis wrote as follows:

> In the district of Ninety-Six, by far the most populous and powerful of the province, Lieutenant-Colonel Balfour, by his great attention and diligence, and by the active assistance of Major Ferguson, who was appointed inspector-general of the militia of this province by Sir Henry Clinton, had formed seven battalions of militia, consisting of above 4,000 men, and entirely composed of persons well affected to the British government, which was so regulated that they could, with ease, furnish 1,500 at a short notice for the defence of the frontier or any other home service. But I must take this opportunity of observing that this militia can be of little use for distant military operations, as they will not stir without a horse; and on that account your Lordship will see the impossibility of keeping a number of them together without destroying the country."

Again, on the 29th, he wrote:

> Ferguson is to move into Tryon county with some militia, whom he says he can depend upon for doing their duty, and fighting well; but I am sorry to say his own experience, as well as that of every other officer, is totally against him."

In view of the above letters, one must agree with the opinion expressed by Sir Henry Clinton, who "could not help being of opinion that the loss of Colonel Ferguson was owing, in a great measure, to Lord Cornwallis having detached Colonel Ferguson with a body of militia without any support of regular troops, notwithstanding, his lordship had informed Sir Henry Clinton—although that brave and zealous officer, judging of himself, had hoped he could make the militia fight without any support of regular troops."

At first all went well. In the words of Captain Chesney, "Colonel Ferguson soon after got intelligence that Colonel McDale (McDowell) was encamped on Cane and Silver Creeks, on which we marched towards the enemy, crossed the winding creek twenty-three times, and found the rebel party strongly posted towards the head of it near the Blue Mountains. We attacked them instantly, and, after a determined resistance, defeated them, and made many prisoners. The rest fled towards Turkey Cove, in order to cross the mountains and get to Holstein."

Ferguson reached Gilbert Town, and halted there for four days. On September 24 he received news that an American force, under Colonel Clarke, had been repulsed at Augusta, and was falling back on North Carolina.

He at once decided to head the enemy off, and pushed out to the West till he was seventy miles from Charlotte. His force now consisted of only 100 men of the American Volunteers and about 1,000 militia, and the enemy finding him thus isolated determined to crush him. In a few days a force of 3,000 backwoodsmen was assembled. Ferguson heard of the enemy's intentions on September 30. He realized the gravity of his position and decided to fall back towards Charlotte. Meanwhile, in the hope of rousing the Loyalists to his assistance, he issued the following proclamation:

> Denard's Ford, Broad River,
> Tryon County,
> October 1, 1780.

Gentleman,

Unless you wish to be eat up by an inundation of barbarians who have begun by murdering an unarmed son before the aged father, and afterwards lopped off his arms, and who, by their shocking cruelties and irregularities, give the best proof of their cowardice and want of discipline:—I say, if you wish to be pinioned, robbed, and murdered, and see your wives and daughters, in four days, abused by the dregs of mankind—in short, if you wish or deserve to live and bear the name of men, grasp your arms in a moment and run to camp.

The Backwater men have crossed the mountains: McDowell, Hampton, Shelby, and Cleveland are at their head: so that you know what you have to depend upon. If you choose to be degraded forever and ever by a set of mongrels, say so at once, and let your women turn their backs upon you, and look out for real men to protect them.

> Pat. Ferguson
> (Major 71st Regiment).

Ferguson sent messages to Cornwallis asking for aid; the following undated letter is believed to have been despatched on October 6:

My Lord

A doubt does not remain with regard to the intelligence I sent your Lordship. They are since joined by Clarke and Sumter,— of course are become an object of some consequence. Happily their leaders are obliged to feed their followers with such hopes, and so to flatter them with accounts of our weakness and fear, that if necessary I should hope for success against them myself: but numbers compared that must be but doubtful.

I am on my march towards you by a road leading from Cherokee Ford north of King's Mountain. Three or four hundred good soldiers, part dragoons, would finish the business. Something must be done soon. This is their last push in this quarter, etc.

Patrick Ferguson.

Meanwhile he had sent orders to the militia to join him at King's Mountain on the boundary of Northern and Southern Carolina, but the Loyalists failed him.

Ferguson reached King's Mountain on October 6. The enemy were all mounted, so it was impossible for Ferguson to avoid an action, and he determined to fight where he was. King's Mountain is a flat-topped hill about 600 yards long, which rises 100 feet above the surrounding country. The top of the hill is only from 60 to 120 yards across, and unfortunately the sides were wooded, and so gave excellent cover to an advancing enemy, except on one side, where there was a precipice.

The small party of American Volunteers were the only men on either side who were armed with a bayonet.

On the 7th a party of 1,500 of the backwoodsmen pushed on and reached King's Mountain at about 4 p.m. They immediately dismounted, tethered their horses, and advanced in three parties up the sides of the hill.

Ferguson said to his men: "Well, boys, here is a place from which all the rebels outside of hell cannot drive us."

The wooded slopes of the hill were a fatal defect in the position, which, in the words of "Light Horse Harry" Lee, was more assailable by the rifle than defensible by the bayonet."

The action that ensued bore a strong resemblance to the fight at Majuba, and is thus described by Captain Chesney:

King's Mountain from its height would have enabled us to oppose a superior force with advantage had it not been covered with wood, which sheltered the Americans and enabled them to fight in their favourite manner. In fact, after driving in our picquets, they were enabled to advance in three divisions, under separate leaders, to the crest of the hill in perfect safety, until they took post, and opened an irregular but destructive fire from behind trees and other cover. Colonel Cleveland's was first perceived, and repulsed by a charge made by Colonel Ferguson; Colonel Selby's next, and met a similar fate, being driven down the hill; lastly, the detachment under Colonel Campbell, and, by desire of Colonel Ferguson, I presented a new front which opposed it with success. By this time the Americans who had been repulsed had regained their former stations, and, sheltered behind trees, poured in an irregular destructive fire.

In this manner the engagement was maintained near an hour, the mountaineers flying when there was danger of being charged by the bayonet, and returning again as soon as the British detachment had faced about to repel another of their parties. Colonel Ferguson was at last recognized by his gallantry, although wearing a hunting shirt, and fell, pierced by seven balls, at the moment he had killed the American Colonel Williams with his left hand, the right being useless.

I had just relieved the troops a second time by Ferguson's orders, when Captain de Peyster succeeded to the command. He soon after sent out a flag of truce; but as the Americans renewed their fire afterwards, ours was also renewed under the supposition that they would give no quarter; and a dreadful havoc took place until the flag was sent out a second time; then the work of destruction ceased. The Americans surrounded us with double lines, and we grounded arms with the loss of one-third of our number.

The American Volunteers behaved with the utmost gallantry, and their casualties amounted to 33 killed and 18 wounded. The Loyalist militia lost above 200 killed and wounded and then gave way. After the surrender the Americans shot down about 100 of their prisoners. As one of their officers put it, "we killed near 100 of the Tories after the surrender of the British, and could hardly be restrained from killing the whole of them."

A few days later they hanged ten of the Loyalist officers at Gilbert Town. On the 10th Tarleton was sent by Cornwallis to assist Ferguson. He discovered another instance of the savagery of the backwoodsmen. In the words of Major Hanger, an officer in Tarleton's Legion:

> The Americans had such an inveteracy against Ferguson, that they buried all the other bodies, but stripped Ferguson's of its clothes, and left it on the field of battle to be devoured by the turkey-buzzards—a species of vulture in that country.

Tarleton describes the action of King's Mountain in the following words:

> The action commenced at four o'clock in the afternoon on the 7th of October, and was disputed with great bravery near an hour, when the death of the gallant Ferguson threw his whole corps into total confusion. No effort was made after this event to resist the enemy's barbarity or revenge the fall of their leader.

The losses of the backwoodsmen only amounted to 28 killed and 60 wounded. King's Mountain was a severe blow to the British cause. Cornwallis at once fell back on Winnsboro, and the Carolina Loyalists never again came forward in any numbers to assist the Royal Army.

Cornwallis acquitted Ferguson of all blame, and reported the disaster in the following words:

> Major Ferguson had taken infinite pains with the militia of Ninety-Six (a frontier post), and had obtained my permission to make an excursion into Tryon County whilst the sickness of my army prevented my moving. As he had only militia and the small remains of his own corps, without baggage or artillery, and as he promised to come back if he heard of any superior forces, I thought he could do no harm, and might help to keep alive the spirit of our friends in North Carolina, which might be depressed by the slowness of our movements. The event proved unfortunate, without any fault of Major Ferguson.
> A numerous and unexpected enemy came from the mountains, and as they had good horses their movements were rapid. Major Ferguson was tempted to stay near them longer than he had intended, in the hope of cutting off Colonel Clarke on his return from Georgia. He was not aware that the enemy was so near him, and in endeavouring to execute my orders of

passing the Catawba and joining me at Charlotte Town he was attacked by a very superior force and totally defeated at King's Mountain.

General Stuart of Garth described Ferguson as follows:

Major Ferguson was brother to Pitfour. He was appointed major to Fraser's Highlanders, but commanded a corps of riflemen which bore his name He possessed original genius, was ardent and enthusiastic, and considered as visionary by the disciples of the mechanical school of war. By zeal animation, and a liberal spirit, he gained the confidence of the mass of the people, and laid foundations on which the loyally disposed, who were numerous in the southern provinces, would have been organized and disciplined and greatly outnumbered the disaffected.

No man in that army was better qualified for such a task; his ardour was not to be checked by common difficulties Directing the conduct of men unaccustomed to strict discipline; instead of commanding obedience, silence, and close attention to the routine of duty, he, with an address which none but a man who studies and applies the principle which regulates the actions of the human mine could be supposed to possess, led them step by step to accomplish the duties of experienced soldiers At King's Mountain he was overpowered by numbers, and fought and fell like a Spartan.

Ferguson had always been conspicuous for his gallantry in action, and in one of his letters he wrote:

I thank God more for this than for all His other blessings, that in every call of danger or honour, I have felt myself collected and equal to the occasion.

As it was not possible to pay any other mark of respect to his memory, some of his friends and brother officers published the following epitaph in the *New York Gazette* of February 14, 1781:

If an ardent thirst for military fame,
A social and benevolent heart,
An uncommon genius,
A mind glowing with patriotic fire,
Replete with useful knowledge,
And capable

Of persevering under difficulties
Where glory was in view,
Claim our admiration;
The fate of
MAJOR PATRICK FERGUSON,
Who possessed these and other virtues
In an eminent degree,
And who fell warring against discord,
Irresistibly
Claims our tears.

MAJOR PATRICK FERGUSON.

Cornet, 2nd Royal North British Dragoons, July 12, 1759.
Captain, 70th Foot, September 1, 1768.
Major, 71st Fraser's Highlanders, October 25, 1779.

8

Medows and Harris

William Medows, the second son of Philip Medows, the deputy-ranger of Richmond Park, and Lady Frances Pierrepont, daughter of the Duke of Kingston, was born on December 31, 1738. In February, 1757, he was gazetted as an ensign in the 50th Foot, then stationed at Maidstone, and he was promoted lieutenant in the following November. He served with his regiment in Germany from June, 1760, till the beginning of 1764, under Prince Ferdinand of Brunswick.

In March, 1764, he became a captain in the 4th Horse (later the 7th Dragoon Guards), and in November, 1766, he was promoted major in the same regiment, which was stationed in Ireland.

On December 31, 1769, Medows was promoted lieutenant-colonel of the 5th Foot. He served with the regiment in the south of Ireland till the autumn of 1773, and acquired a great liking for young Harris. In 1770 he married France; daughter of Robert Hammerton, of Hammerton Co. Tipperary.

George Harris was the eldest son of Rev. George Harris, curate of Brasted in Kent. His father was the youngest of a family of seven children.

George was born on March 18, 1746, and he was educated at Westminster. His father obtained for him from Lord George Sackville a nomination as a cadet at the Royal Military Academy, Woolwich, in January, 1759. Towards the close of this year his father died, and George now found himself in the care of his maternal uncle, Rev. Michael Bull, the rector of Brasted. In due course he was appointed a lieutenant-fireworker in the artillery, but on the advice and with the assistance of the Marquess of Granby he left the artillery and became an ensign in the 6th Foot in July, 1762.

He joined the regiment at Bedford early in March, 1763, and soon

WILLIAM MEDOWS

afterwards saved the life of a brother officer, who had fallen into the Ouse while boating.

In January, 1765, young Harris purchased his step, and it is interesting to note that at this time he not only lived on his pay but even saved some money.

In September, 1767, he was appointed adjutant of his regiment, and exactly a year later he obtained leave, and went over to France to study the language. He remained abroad for five months, and returned to England at the end of February, 1769. After a short stay in England, young Harris rejoined his regiment at Limerick, and not long afterwards he went to Cashel with a detachment. On Christmas Eve he was dining four miles from Cashel. A tremendous snowstorm came on, and he could not return. He reported his arrival in barracks long before parade on Christmas morning, but the officer commanding the detachment first ordered him to his quarters, and then called him out without seconds and fired at him twice. The officer was mad, and died in confinement not long afterwards, This was a somewhat unconventional way of spending Christmas Day!

Harris spent the year 1770 in Ireland, but in July, 1771, he purchased his company, and proceeded on recruiting duty to England. In 1773 he was back with his regiment in Kinsale, and in September of that year Lieutenant-Colonel Medows was transferred to the 12th Light Dragoons, so the two officers were parted for a time.

In May, 1774, the 5th Foot was ordered to America, and Captain Harris announced the news to a cousin of his in the following letter:

Kinsale,
May, 1774.

My Dear Bess,

How vain are the best-laid schemes for mortal happiness without the concurrence of the All-seeing Power! The very morning I had leave for two years at least came an order for the regiment to go to Boston, every officer to attend. The transports are arrived, and we expect to be or board on Monday, if not sooner; so, most probably, ere this reaches you, your George will have been most heartily sick, and on the mend again.

The regiment remained at Boston, and was kept hard at work. On December 5 Captain Harris wrote again to his cousin:

I shall not attempt to lengthen this letter, as I have to write by tomorrow night to my mother, besides making love, and at-

GEORGE HARRIS

tending a field-day, which we have as often as possible, firing ball constantly, so we shall at least be prepared for these wrong-headed people.

Things continued like this for four months longer. Harris was now the senior captain in the 5th Foot, and commanded the grenadier company.

On April 19, 1775, General Gage sent off the flank companies to seize and destroy some stores at Concord, and this brought on the action of Lexington. In the retirement Harris had half his company killed or wounded his subaltern—being wounded. Lord Percy, the colonel of the 5th Foot, was sent out with four battalions and ten companies of Marines to extricate the flank companies. Only 1,800 British troops took part in this affair, and there were 269 casualties.

There was now another lull. The British took advantage of this opportunity to strengthen their position at Boston, but provisions were not very plentiful, and on May 5 Harris wrote:

At present, it should seem we have the worst of the fight, for, however we block up their port, the rebels certainly block up our town, and have cut off our good beef and mutton, much to the discomfort of our mess.

From the following letter it appears that, a month later, food was still more scarce, and the army was getting impatient for action:

Grenadier Camp,
June 12, 1775.

Affairs at present wear a serious aspect. I wish the Americans may be brought to a sense of their duty. One good drubbing, which I long to give them, by way of retaliation, might have a good effect towards it. At present they are so elated by the petty advantage they gained the 19th of April, that they despise the power of Britain, who seems determined to exert herself in the conflict. Troops every day coming in, and such as will soon enable us, I hope, to take the field on the other side the Demel, *alias* the Neck. At present we are completely blockaded, and subsisting almost on salt provision, except such as the Americans (so strong is the old leaven of smuggling in them, about which these troubles arose) bring into us.

My garden (*a propos* to gardens, you and I will certainly have one)—what can afford the philosophic mind such food for contemplation?—with salt provisions, what can afford such food for the body? such salads such excellent greens the young turnip-tops make? Then the spinach and radishes, with the cucumbers, beans, and peas, so promising. All within six weeks from the firs turning of the soil, is really surprising. Jonathan is an excellent gardener, though this is his first essay. I was quite Uncle Toby; to plan and to direct was my department, his to execute and improve.

My house will be struck over my head if I do not quit it, as a change of ground is to take place immediately. I only wish the movement was towards the Americans, that we might sooner bring this unpleasant business to an issue, and get home to our friends. Near three years since I left you, and but little probability that three year more will bring me back. But a soldier should not complain, and I think, Bess, that yours will be one of the last to do so. The ground is marked out Holmes says we shall be last, so *adieu*. May we, to the last, preserve that friendship that has hitherto been so pleasant to both.

Remember me to all friends,

Yours, etc.,

G. Harris.

Holmes was soldier-servant to Captain Harris.

On June 17 occurred the famous Battle of Bunker's Hill. Harris was severely wounded in the head, and he described the events of the day as follows:

We had made a breach in their fortifications, which I had twice mounted, encouraging the men to follow me, and was ascending a third time, when a ball grazed the top of my head, and I fell, deprived of sense and motion. My Lieutenant, Lord Rawdon, caught me in his arms, and, believing me dead, endeavoured to remove me from the spot, to save my body from being trampled on. The motion, while it hurt me, restored my senses, and I articulated: 'For God's sake, let me die in peace.'

The hope of preserving my life induced Lord Rawdon to order four soldiers to take me up, and carry me to a place of safety. Three of them were wounded while performing this office (one afterwards died of his wounds), but they succeeded in placing me under some trees out of the reach of the balls. A retreat having been sounded, poor Holmes was running about like a madman in search of me, and luckily came to the place where I lay just in time to prevent my being left behind; for when they brought me to the water's edge the last boat was put off, the men calling out they 'would take no more.'

On Holmes hallooing out, 'It is Captain Harris,' they put back and took me in. I was very weak and faint, and seized with a severe shivering Our blankets had been flung away during the engagement; luckily there was one belonging to a man in the boat, in which wrapping me up and laying me in the bottom, they conveyed me safely to my quarters.

The surgeons did not at first apprehend danger from the contusion, notwithstanding the extreme pain I felt, which increased very much if I attempted to lie down. A worthy woman seeing this lent me an easy chair, but this being full of bugs only added to my sufferings. My agonies increasing, and the surgeons observing symptoms of matter forming (which, had it fallen on the brain, must have produced instant death or at least distraction), performed the operation of trepanning, from which time the pain abated and I began to recover; but before the callous was formed they indulged me with the gratification of a singular curiosity—fixing looking-glasses so as to give me a sight of my own brain.

The heat of the weather and the scarcity of fresh provisions added greatly to the sufferings of the wounded. As patience was the only remedy for the former, I trusted to it for relief; and for the latter, the attention of the surgeon, and a truly benevolent family in Boston, who supplied me with mutton-broth, when no money could purchase it was a blessing for which I can never be sufficiently thankful

As soon as his wound was dressed, he wrote a short note to reassure his mother; and he always preserved a silver button which had belonged to the grenadier who was killed while carrying him off.

By July 24 he was so far recovered from his wound that he was able to write the following letter to his cousin:

Very unwillingly should I let this opportunity slip of telling my dear Bess that I am in a fair way perfectly to recover from the consequence of my wound; indeed, fortune seems to intend you shall have a few lines from me, as the vessel has been detained from the date of my letter to my mother till now. When

I wrote to her my hand trembled so much that I fear that she would conclude me to be worse than I really was, but this was occasioned by weakness from lying in bed, and not by pain, from which I was relieved almost entirely as soon as the operation was performed. What I suffered before that I alone can know! They still every day peep at my brain, which, all things considered, is not an unlucky circumstance, as it may convince you and the rest of the world that I have such a thing; and I should not regret that you and the rest of my friends in old England could, in the same manner, take a peep at my heart. I am convinced they would find a warmth of affection they may more imagine than I can describe.

So much for lectures on heads and hearts. Next, let me paint, in a few words, our present agreeable situation, first apologizing to my dear and best of mothers for not having said more on the head, owing to weakness and restriction—indeed I am now rather exceeding bounds. The situation of Boston will be better explained to you by a common map than by my description. The whole circle from Charlestown Neck to Dorchester is one continued fortification, to all appearance lined with the Americans, so that every avenue to the country is effectually shut, and not one bit of any kind of provisions do they suffer to be brought in, which obliges us to subsist on salt provisions, without even vegetables—pleasant, you may think, in the hot sun.

As a sick person I am confined to broth alone. But broth of salt pork? that's impossible. Yes, we get sometimes a piece of an old ox or cow at the rate of fourteen times as much as we paid last summer, and from an extraordinary return to civility, one of the surgeons of the general hospital has most kindly supplied me, every two or three days, with mutton sufficient to make me an excellent mess of broth. Would not you and my mother kiss him for his kindness? At least I shall tell him so.

I have heard a piece of news that I could wish confirmed *i.e.,* the Colonists have an answer from England to the affair of the 19th April that you are determined to withdraw all troops from the Colonies, and carry on the war by sea only. This appears the only possible way of distressing them as we can cut off every intercourse with other nations, and by that means bring them to reason at a much smaller expense than it can possibly be effected by land; then we shall have the pleasure of revisiting Old England once more. A circumstance that would give me great pleasure; for, though I am ready with life and limb to execute the orders of my King, yet, when the business can be better done, without running my head against a post, I am not one of those bloody-minded people that wish only for revenge and slaughter. I have scribbled the paper full, and have only just room to tell you the opinion of the faculty, on the last dressing which I can have before the ship sails, and to assure you I am, with the greatest truth,

> Your affectionate friend,
>
> G. Harris.

P.S.—Everything about my old pate goes on as it should do.

Sir William Howe promised to get a commission for Thomas, the younger brother of Captain Harris, who wrote once more to his cousin on October 8, apparently in great spirits:

> We have had great promotion going on, and if the war lasts another campaign, shall have more. My situation, not my services, entitles me to expect something from Fortune. Perhaps she may think another rap on the pate sufficient. Be that as it may
>
> *I'll keep, tho' in the midst of woe,*
> *Myself in equilibrio.'*
>
> As for politics, I know nothing about them; but judging from appearances, there is reason to expect a longer war.

Almost immediately after writing this letter Captain Harris returned to England on recruiting duty. His stay at home was short, but it was now that he first met the lady whom he afterwards married. On May 24, 1776, he sailed once more from Portsmouth, accompanied by his brother Thomas, who had been gazetted ensign in the 5th Foot.

The brothers reached America just in time for Sir William Howe's New York campaign.

In accordance with the usual custom, the flank companies of all the regiments were formed into separate battalions, and Captain Harris found that his company formed part of a battalion of grenadiers commanded by Lieutenant-Colon Medows, who had been transferred to the 55th Foot in September, 1775.

Harris described the campaign in the following letter to his uncle:

On 5th August we made the harbour of New York, and at the entrance joined the very fleet with which I had so much wished to sail, and of which ours, in fact, was the second part.

On the 18th I got quit of the recruits to my great satisfaction, and joined my company on Staten Island. About the 20th we embarked in boats for Long Island, and landed, without opposition, in Gravesend Bay; marched six miles inland, and halted till the 26th. A large body of the Americans near us kept up a fire from behind walls and trees. About 4 p.m. of the 26 we struck tents, and lay on our arms during the night about three miles from Bedford; and though in summer, it was the coldest night I had experienced up to this time (25th November).

Such sudden changes of climate are not uncommon here. The weather is now most unnaturally hot and close, after severe frosts.

At daybreak, the 27th, the light infantry attacked and forced several small posts which the Americans had on the road leading to their lines at Bedford. This appeared to be the first notice they had of our being near to them. About nine we fired two signal guns to a part of the army under General Grant, who was to make a feint in the front of the Americans, while we got round to their rear; and immediately marched briskly up to them, when, almost without firing a shot, they abandoned their post, and retreated to their lines under cover of their guns (these they also evacuated two or three days after, retiring upon New York during the night).

Our men were most eager to attack them in their lines, and I am convinced would have carried them, but we were ordered to retreat out of reach of their guns, and lay from about 4 p.m. till very near dark at the entrance of a small wood, exposed to the fire of their riflemen. During the whole evening they hit but one man, though their balls continually whistled over our heads, and lodged in the trees above us. Their loss that day is acknowledged by them to have been 2,600; ours about 300 in killed and wounded.

In a letter to his cousin, he refers as follows to the Battle of Brooklyn:

We have had what some call a battle, but if it deserves that name, it was the pleasantest I ever heard of, as we had not received more than a dozen shot from the enemy, when they ran away with the utmost precipitation. You may imagine the eagerness of our brave fellows. We have cleared Long Island, and I think, in a day or two, shall be on the continent. The contents of this letter are to be communicated in Marlborough Street, as I cannot find time to write more than once in our present state of hurry. The paper I write on was once the property of an American, at least so I suppose, as it was brought to me by my corporal.

Colonel Medows is my commanding officer, and this I consider one of the pleasantest things that ever happened to me. We sleep together in a soldiers' tent, which, when well littered down with straw, we consider quite a luxury. He led us on to action in the most gallant manner; and I am convinced that if General Howe had made a sign for us to follow the Americans into their works, we would have done it. Thanks to the general's prudence, we have effected this object without the loss of the many brave fellows who must have fallen in the attempt.

We will now resume the letter to his uncle:

On the 30th the reserve, with the light infantry, again left the army, which the next day took peaceable possession of all the American works on Long Island, and encamped near Hell Gate.

Batteries were soon erected to oppose a work they had on York Island, and though the East River is there 800 paces across, our Artillery soon silenced theirs, and, as we afterwards found, dismounted most of their guns. Our landing on York Island was effected without the loss of a man, for the moment they saw us ashore they retreated to their works at Kingsbridge.

A lieutenant of theirs, who was that night my prisoner, informed me that a body of 3,000 had got round to our right, with the intention of attacking us before we could form after landing, but so little eager were they to commence the assault, that upon their falling in with two companies of grenadiers, who had by accident been posted on the same road, they fled with the utmost haste; not even taking time to put on their packs and blankets, which they had thrown off on a thorough conviction of beating us. Their blankets were a great prize, as several of our men had thrown off theirs on the 27th, when pursuing the enemy. Here they amply made up their losses.

I wish that Tom were with us, and as my lieutenant. At present he makes war with a thousand luxuries, of which we are deprived. These, however, he cares as little for as I do, and the other night wished to volunteer going with us to attack in the Jerseys, but was prevented doing so. You may be sure I did not throw cold water on his offer, but rejoiced in it, and should have been as happy to have had him fighting by my side as to see him making successful love to Miss ———.

After landing on York Island, we drove the Americans into their works beyond the eighth mile-stone from New York, and thus got possession of the best half of the island. We took post opposite to them, placed our picquets, borrowed a sheep, killed, cooked, and ate some of it, and then went to sleep on a gate, which we took the liberty of throwing off its hinges, covering our feet with an American tent, for which we should have cut poles and pitched, had it not been so dark. Give me such living as we enjoy at present, such a hut and such company, and I would not care three farthings if we stayed all the winter, for though the mornings and evenings are cold, yet the sun is so hot as to oblige me to put up a blanket as a screen.

Tell my best of mothers that my compass has been of the greatest use in enabling me to ascertain the proper aspects for our houses, and has gained me, in fine, the thanks of all parties.

The 16th of September we were ordered to stand to our arms at 11 a.m., and were instantly trotted about three miles (without a halt to draw breath), to support a battalion of light infantry, which had imprudently advanced so far without support as to be in great danger of being cut off. This must have happened but for our haste. So dangerous a quality is courage without prudence for its guide; with it, how noble and respectable it makes the man! But to return to our narrative The instant the front of our columns appeared, the enemy began to retire to their works, and our light infantry to their camp.

On our return we were exposed to the fire of the Americans. A man in my company had his hat shot through nearly in the direction of my wound, but the ball merely raised the skin; and in the battalion on our left a man was shot so dead when lying on the ground, that the next man did not perceive it, but when he got up to stand to his arms, kicked his comrade, thinking he was asleep, and then found, to his great surprise, that he was quite dead, a ball having entered under the ear, and very little blood having issued from it.

Before we started in the morning, our dinner, consisting of a goose and piece of mutton, had been put on the fire. The moment we marched, our domestic deposited the above-named delicacies on a chaise and followed us with it to our ground. When the fight was over, he again hung the goose to the fire, but the poor bird had scarcely been half done, when we were ordered to return to our station. There we again commenced cooking, and, though without dish, plate, or knife, did ample justice to our fare, which we washed down with bad rum and water, and then composed ourselves to rest on our friendly gate. Our baggage joined us next day.

We remained in camp till the 10th October, waiting for redoubts to be formed across the island. Lord Percy was left to defend these, with three brigades of British, and Hearne's brigade of Hessians. At 8 p.m. of the 10th, the reserve, the light infantry, and 1,500 Hessians, embarked in boats, under General Clinton, went up to the East River, passed Hell Gate, and landed at Frogneck without opposition. I cannot here help noticing a part of the river we went through, called Devil's Pans, at the point of an island, which here divides the river into two rapid streams, and causes a very dangerous whirlpool. The suction is so great, that at times the river on that side is impassable.

This danger we avoided, though with difficulty, for, through the ignorance of our pilot, we were on the edge of the pool when too late to avoid the suction, and found ourselves, circle after circle attracted to the centre in spite of all our efforts, till at last the boatmen were on the point of quitting their oars, despairing of escape, when, animated I suppose by the love of life, I began to storm at them for their cowardice, and made them stick to their oars. We at length perceived that we made progress, and emerged from the whirlpool, escaping without other accident than the dislocation of a man's wrist, who very foolishly attempted to fend off a large wherry containing fifty men, which, by the force of the stream, was carried against our boat.

We lay on Frogneck till the 10th of October; on the 18th, at one in the morning, the van of the army, consisting of the light infantry and grenadiers, embarked for the continent, and landed without opposition. The boats soon brought over great part of the army, when we marched into the country, drove the enemy from some posts, and lay on our arms near New Rochelle. We lost here two light infantry officers and some men, owing to their too great haste to attack. The grenadiers did not suffer, being only exposed to the fire of the American batteries, which were very ill served. From this we marched to White Plains, being informed that 15,000 American troops were entrenched there.

On the 28th, the army, in two columns, marched towards their position, and here, for the first time, we were tranquil spectators of the fight, except, indeed, as far as our anxiety for our friends and comrades was concerned. I had a brother in peril, till then unknown to him. Thanks to God that he behaved like a man, and escaped unhurt. May he ever display the same spirit with the same result!

The Americans behaved in the most dastardly manner, for though they at first made a show of resistance, no sooner was our second brigade ordered to advance, than they gave way with such precipitation, that they escaped to the heights before our men could reach them. They acknowledge, however, to have lost in killed and wounded 600; ours was 200. Two days after this engagement they abandoned the heights, without attempting to defend them.

On the 5th of November we commenced our retreat from White Plains, and marched very leisurely to Fort Washington, on New York Island. After some halts, we were ordered on the 16th of November to attack the neighbouring heights, prparatory to investing it, which we very soon effected, and ere landing received terms of capitulation from the commandant of the fort, which some days before they declared was to have prevented us from returning that way to New York. Here we took 2,500 prisoners.

On the 19th of November we again struck tents, and embarked in boats at Fort Washington, passed Fort Constitution without being perceived, and landed at a place four miles above it, where 100 resolute men might have stopped our whole army. Here we took possession of their tents, baggage, thirty-two guns, and a great quantity of stores.

We now pursued the enemy much too slowly for our wishes;

but it is not for us subordinates to comment on the movements of our commanders, of which we are in general very incompetent judges. Warped by passion, we consider only visible objects, and forget the thousand latent wheels by which a great army moves.

We marched *via* Newbridge, Newark, and Elizabeth Town, to New Brunswick. So soon as winter quarters are settled, I depart for New York, where all my effects are in store, but where I most heartily wish they had never gone, as they will, in all probability, be greatly damaged. However, life is left, and if the war continue, I have prospects that will amply repay for such losses; and if fair peace should come, she's welcome, for I shall then return to my dearest friends, and be, though poor, contented.

The Americans have crossed the Delaware, and give out that they mean to attack us on the other side. Next spring will put them to the test. Till then, *adieu* politics and military operations; unless, indeed, a winter campaign should take place, of which there is some idea. I must not omit to inform you of the capture of Colonel Lee. He was taken by a party of ours, under Colonel Harcourt, who surrounded the house in which this arch-traitor was residing. Lee behaved as cowardly in this transaction as he had dishonourably in every other.

After firing one or two shots from the house, he came out and entreated our troops to spare his life. Had he behaved with proper spirit, I should have pitied him, and wished that his energies had been exerted in a better cause. I could hardly refrain from tears when I first saw him, and thought of the miserable fate in which his obstinacy has involved him. He says he has been mistaken in three things:

Firstly, That the New England men would fight; secondly, That America was unanimous; and thirdly, That she could afford two men for our one.—*Adieu.*

On December 26 occurred the regrettable incident at Trenton. Captain Harris describes the affair in the following letter. His adventures when going to the Americans with a flag of truce are of interest. In quite recent times officers sometimes found taking a flag of truce to an irregular enemy an expensive and unpleasant duty, when they were forced to return, deprived not only of their horses but of every stitch of clothing they stood up in.

You know from history, reverses in war are not uncommon. To have had our successes continued totally uninterrupted was, perhaps, more than the most sanguine Tory ever expected. Till very lately Caesar's laconic '*Veni, vidi, vici,*' might justly have been used by us. Had I time I would attempt to relate the whole affair at Trenton as it passed, according to the best information we could collect. But you must be contented with a slight sketch. We understand that Colonel Rawle, who commanded the Hessians, had intelligence of the intended attack, and had his men under arms the whole night.

Long after daybreak, a most violent storm of snow coming on, he thought he might safely permit his men to lie down, and in this state they were surprised by the enemy. The Hessian were about 1,300; between 800 and 900 were taken, the rest escaping by a road, by which nearly the whole might have got off, if, in those moments every man had been collected. But this is not to be expected. This success gave the American such spirit that they crossed the river in numbers sufficient to make a post of Hessians fall back to Prince Town, and even then to cause such an alarm as led the commanding officer to request reinforcement. This was not complied with for some days, but then a part of the army was sent the grenadiers, with the second battalion of Guards.

You would have felt too much to be able to express your feelings, on seeing with what warmth of friendship our children, as we call the light infantry, welcomed us, one and all crying 'Let them come!' 'Lead us to them, we are sure of being supported!' It gave me a pleasure to fine to attempt expressing, and if you see a stain on the paper, pray place the drops to the right motive, for the tears flowed even at the thought, so that I could not stop them. This reverse has given the Americans great spirits, which I am convinced they never would have had if the Hessians had not been surprised, but fought as I have seen them.

Washington, to do him justice, has taken advantage of the moment, crossing the Delaware, and beating three regiments that lay in his way. This has elated them so much, and occasioned such a change of quarters in our army, as to render the prospect of passing the winter in ease and luxury totally dark. The country which was entirely our own being now divided between us;

and everything which was then to be got for money and at very moderate prices must now be earned at the point of the sword, and, what is worse, with very great fatigue.

I could tell you a long story of an excursion of mine to the rebel army, but, as I did not see their commander, the rest is not worthy of description. I shall therefore merely say that Lord Cornwallis employed me to carry a letter to General Washington relative to the Hessians' prisoners, and I returned safe, to the astonishment of most of my friends, with the two light horse who accompanied me. It may appear extraordinary that with a flag of truce I should be in danger, but the whole country is full of their scouting parties, whose greatest ambition is to be behind a cover and kill our light dragoons, who patrol most of the roads at different times, and for whose heads, it is said, a reward is offered in the army.

However, in a few miles' riding I found all the same parties so much more afraid of us than we were of them, that we hallooed and laughed at several who, on first seeing us, took to their heels. I must now bid you *adieu* and go my rounds.

For several months no event of importance took place. The 5th Foot formed part of the force which sailed from New York under Sir William Howe on July 23, 1777, and landed at Elk Bay on the Chesapeake on August 25. As usual, the flank companies were formed with separate battalions.

On September 3 Captain Harris was wounded in the leg at the action of Iron Hill.

The Battle of Brandywine took place eight days later. Captain Harris was in a chaise with the baggage on account of his wound, but he secured a horse, joined his Grenadiers, and took part in the battle. Lieutenant-Colonel Medows, who commanded the battalion of grenadiers, had his right arm broken by a bullet while leading on his men. The ball then entered his body and knocked him off his horse, and the fall broke his left collar-bone. Harris went up to him as he lay. The colonel could not use either hand, and exclaimed, "It's hard," and then at once added, "It's lucky, Harris, poor Fanny does not know this."

After the action Captain Harris's wound became worse, so both he and Colonel Medows were sent down to Wilmington, and missed the Battle of Germantown on October 4. In this engagement the colonel of the 5th Foot was mortally wounded, and he died two days later. In consequence of this Harris was promoted major on October 7. Soon afterwards he was able to rejoin the army at Philadelphia, and he found himself in command of the 5th Foot. Colonel Medows was brought back to the 5th Foot, but his wounds prevented him from joining.

Major Harris remained with his regiment at Philadelphia until the town was evacuated on June 18, 1778, and he covered the embarkation at Sandy Hook on July 5. The army moved across to New York.

On February 6, 1778, France had concluded a treaty with the Americans and joined in the war against England; and in July a French fleet appeared off the mouth of the Delaware with 4,000 troops on board.

Then as now both France and England held islands in the West Indies. Among the Windward Islands, St. Lucia, Martinique, and Guadeloupe, belonged to France, while Barbadoes, Grenada, St. Vincent, and Dominica, were English.

The French began the war in the West Indies by the seizure of Dominica in September, 1778. Clinton was ordered to despatch a force to capture the French islands. General Grant was selected for the command. He was given ten battalions (5,800 men), which were embarked in fifty-nine transports. The fleet did not sail from New York till November 4, but, as was very usual in those days, the troops were embarked several weeks before-hand. The destination of the force was kept secret, and on October 15 Major Harris wrote as follows to his cousin:

> If anyone should ask you where I am going, tell them what, by the way of a secret, I'll tell you,—I do not know—and, if they should be more inquisitive, that I do not care. But, at the same time, say I am on the tip-top of Fortune's wheel, and that, if they want to write to me, they may direct to Major Harris, commander of the grenadiers, second in command under Brigadier-General Medows. Tell my best of mothers my happiness, and let her pray that her spirit may not fail me in the day of trial. Everyone seems to think our expedition is the road home; if we can only get hand to hand with the *Monsieurs*, I am convinced it will be a glorious one."

The expedition reached Barbadoes on December 10, and anchored in Cul de Sac Bay in the island of St. Lucia, on the afternoon of the 12th. Grant at once landed two brigades and secured the heights.

Next morning Medows landed with the reserve, which consisted of the 5th Foot together with the Grenadiers and Light companies of the whole force, and took possession of the Vigie, on the north side of Castries Bay.

In these less formal days the somewhat pompous order which General Medows issued on assuming command of the reserve makes quaint reading:

St. Lucie. Reserve Orders. December 14, 1778.
Brigadier-General Medows is extremely sensible of the high honour conferred upon him by being appointed to so distinguished a corps as the reserve. From the gallant activity of the Light Infantry, the determined bravery of the Grenadiers, and the confirmed discipline of the 5th Regiment, everything is to be expected.
The troops are desired to remember that clemency should go hand in hand with bravery, that an enemy in our power is an enemy no more, and the glorious characteristic of a British soldier is to conquer and to spare. Acting on these principles they can never fail doing honour to themselves, their King, and the country they serve.

The reserve had scarcely landed, when the French fleet under the Marquis D'Estaing, with 9,000 troops on board, hove in sight. D'Estaing could not effect a landing in Cul de Sac Bay, but on the 15th he landed his force in the Anse du Choc, and decided to fall upon the British and beat them in detail. His first objective was the detached reserve on the Vigie, under Medows.

The Vigie was connected with the mainland by an isthmus only 200 yards across.

Medows drew up the bulk of his force in rear of this neck, but by means of an advanced post, occupied by five of his light companies, he made it impossible for the French general to pen him in the Vigie and march on to attack Grant.

On the morning of the 18th, 12,000 French troops attacked the Vigie, and after a desperate conflict, lasting three hours, they fell back shattered and discomfited by a British force only 1,300 strong. The following account of the action was written by Lord Harris a few years before his death:

As some proof of what we were, allow me to relate the conduct of two of my companies as a specimen of the battalion, and, indeed, of the detachment. My gallant friend, now no more, Captain Shawe, with the 4th Company, was ordered by me to make his men lie down, and cover themselves in the brushwood as much as possible, to prevent them being seen as marks; when he (still standing as conspicuous as when he crossed the bank of the *nullah* before Seringapatam in April, 1799) immediately assured me he could answer that not a man would even wish to stir until I ordered them.

In this situation he had eight killed and wounded out of fifty, without firing a shot! To show the steadiness of the battalion, on my ordering the 35th Company,[1] commanded by Captain Massey (from a reserve of three companies which I kept under cover of a small eminence), to relieve the 49th Company, he was in an instant at his post, and as quickly ordered the company to make ready, and had given them the word 'Present!' when I called out: 'Captain Massey, my orders were not to fire; recover!'

This was done without a shot, and themselves under a heavy fire. This will, I trust, prove our colour was right British; and may it not be deemed an interference of Providence that, when we took possession of the Vigie, the enemy should have retired with such precipitation as to leave two twelve-pounders unspiked, with many rounds of ammunition? These guns certainly determined the fate of the day, being most ably managed by our senior artillery officer, Lieutenant ———. Alas! I cannot recall his name, although I so well remember his ingenuous praise of my beloved brother, and his active gallantry and masterly management of the two twelve-pounders; nor can I forget Hill's and my disappointment when he lugged upon his shoulder a box of ammunition from the water-side, so heavy that it took two men to each of the same weight to follow him with their burden.

---

1. In Lushington's *Life of Lord Harris* this reads "the 45th Company," but the grenadier company of the 45th did not take part in this expedition, whereas the 35th Regiment was present.

According to Fortescue's *History of the British Army*, "the grenadier company of the 35th did not form part of the reserve, and so was not present at the Vigie; but the evidence on this point seems conclusive, for Lieutenant Thomas Williams, the subaltern of the grenadier company, was wounded at the Vigie.

Moreover, at that date there were only two captains named Massey in the British Army namely, Captain F. H. Massey, of the 5th Dragoons (then stationed in Ireland); and Captain Hugh Massey, of the 35th Foot.

He threw it down, and on opening it we found the cartridges so rotten that on being handled they crumbled to dust. We had but three rounds left; I turned to husband them, and he to join the 5th again, neither saying a word.

What immediately followed cannot be better expressed than in Sir William Medows's own words, repeated to me many years after the action:

> A few minutes before my giving you my last order, I considered it all over with us! You had scarcely whispered to me we had not three rounds a man left, when a shot took you that I thought must be fatal. My wound was becoming very painful; their column rapidly advancing; the wounded from our line constantly passing to the hospital; all looked ill. But your running up the little eminence the shot had driven you from gave me hopes again, and I left you to prepare for my part in the orders I gave you. These were for you to charge with the line when you thought the enemy sufficiently near, and then all that could scramble off to join me at the flagstaff, from which I could charge with you as the last effort, and conquer or fall!

I proceeded accordingly to the front of our line to prepare for the charge, when, to my great joy, I saw the head of the enemy's column staggering, and some men even turned to retreat, from the effect of two rounds of the twelve-pounders. I instantly ordered the companies near me to fire, bidding them direct upon those in confusion, and in a minute or two the whole column was gone about, and retreating as fast as their sense of honour would allow—a feeling that the gallant soldier has even to death, that his enemy may not disgrace him with the name of a runaway.

At the crisis of the fight, when ammunition was running short, Medows addressed the men of the 5th Foot in the following words: "Soldiers, as long as you have a bayonet to point against an enemy's breast, defend these colours."

In his official despatch about the action, General Grant said that the attacks were delivered "with the impetuosity of Frenchmen, and repulsed with the determined bravery of Britons."

The casualties of the British were only 13 killed and 158 wounded.

Medows himself was severely wounded in the right arm early in the action, and Lieutenant Thomas Harris was mortally wounded. Fortunately, Major Harris was merely bruised by a spent bullet.

The British infantry behaved magnificently, and the results of their war training in America were conspicuous. The losses of the French were 400 killed and 1,200 wounded, a total of casualties which far exceeded the number of English muskets. In spite of his wound, General Medows did not give up command of the reserve, and on Christmas Day he issued the following order:

St.Lucie. Reserve Orders. December 25, 1778.

As soon as our gallant and generous enemy are seen to advance in great numbers, the troops are to receive them with three huzzas, and then to be perfectly silent and obedient to their officers.

Whilst they are cool by day and alert by night, they have nothing to fear. If the enemy want our arms, let them come and take them.

During the attack the drums and fifes are to assemble round the colours of the 5th Regiment and beat the '*Grenadiers' March.*'

D'Estaing now withdrew to Martinique, and left the British in possession of St. Lucia.

A letter from Major Harris to his mother about the death of her younger son contained the following sentence:

Queens might behold you with envy, mourning as a mother for such a son.

And on March 14 he wrote as follows to his cousin:

Even the flinty heart of a soldier could not tell me of his death, but called General Medows aside, who, with tears that almost stopped his utterance, stammered out: 'Harris, be a man in this, as in everything else; the struggle is past.' 'Tis impossible to convey to you the obligation I owe General Medows, or the love I bear him. He is brave, good, and generous."

The 5th Foot expected to be sent home very soon, and in June Major Harris wrote:

Five campaigns, though they have not abated my zeal, have certainly tended to strengthen my original love of retirement. A country life, with land enough to give me employment, is what

I have, however distant the prospect, continually in view.

Soon after this the regiment was embarked on the fleet as marines, and took part in a naval action with the French off Grenada. Major Harris now got leave, and sailed for England in a Dutch vessel. The ship was captured by a French privateer, but the officers on board were released after a short detention in France; for it had been agreed between the two nations that officers taken in neutral vessels were not to be considered prisoners of war. On December 9 he married Ann, the daughter of Mr. Charles Dixon, of Bath, and soon afterwards he returned with his wife to his regiment, which was now in Barbadoes.

Mrs. Harris returned to England early in the summer of 1780; and the regiment followed soon after, and reached Plymouth in September.

In the year 1780 Colonel Medows returned to England, and was appointed Colonel of the 89th Regiment. In January, 1781, he was made a local Major-General, and given the command of four battalions with which to seize the Cape of Good Hope. The transports were escorted by a squadron under Commodore Johnstone, and sailed in March. Johnstone was attacked at Porto Praya, in the Cape Verde Islands, by a French squadron under Suffren on April 16th, and as a successful attempt on the Cape of Good Hope was no longer practicable, he decided to return home with his frigates while the transports proceeded under escort to India. Medows, who had been promoted Major-General in November, 1782, landed at Madras on February 17, 1783. He took part in some desultory operations against Mysore. In July news reached India of the peace between England and France, but the war with Tipu dragged on till March, 1784. Shortly after the conclusion of peace General Medows returned to England.

In December, 1780, Harris was promoted lieutenant-colonel, and ordered to Ireland with his regiment. They had a very rough passage, and were nearly wrecked on the Old Head of Kinsale. Harris spent the next six years in Ireland, but when the 5th Foot was placed under orders for America he determined to sell out and settle down at home.

Everything was arranged, and Harris went to London to receive the money for his commission, when an accidental meeting with Major-General Medows in St. James's Street altered his plans.

Medows asked whether the king had actually signed the new commission, and on hearing he had not done so, he said:

Then, Harris, you shan't sell out—you shall go with me as secretary and *aide-de-camp*; I am just appointed governor of Bombay, and your presence will be a host to me. I'll go directly to the agent and stop the sale.

Instead of selling out, Lieutenant-Colonel Harris exchanged, in October, 1787, into the 76th Foot, then serving in India; and General Medows advanced him 4,000 to insure his life for the benefit of his wife and children.

Medows and Harris sailed for the East early in 1788, and reached Bombay in September. General Medows was governor and commander-in-chief of Bombay until he was transferred to Madras in January, 1790. He left the entire management of his money affairs in the hands of Colonel Harris.

General Medows did not have long to settle down in Madras before the outbreak of the third Mysore War. Colonel Harris accompanied the General throughout the campaign.

On May 26 Medows advanced from Trichinopoly with 15,000 men, and by the end of July he had occupied Karur, Darapuram, and Coimbatore. In a few more weeks the British forces had taken Palghaut and Dindigul and occupied Erode. These enterprises, however, had entailed a dangerous dispersion of the troops, and in September Tipu struck. He recaptured Darapuram, reoccupied Erode, and avoiding Medows, who moved out after him from Coimbatore, he advanced to Trichinopoly and ravaged the country. The arrival of General Medows on December 14 caused Tipu to retire to Mysore, and Medows then returned to Madras.

On the whole the campaign had proved a failure. Lord Cornwallis, the governor-general, now decided to assume the command in person, so that in the subsequent operations Medows was only a subordinate.

At the capture of the town of Bangalore, on March 7, 1791, Medows, having nothing to do, accompanied the storming-party. As a slender subaltern crawled through a narrow gap in the wall, Medows called out to the grenadiers of the 36th Foot, "Well done! Now, Whiskers, support the little gentleman."

In the action at Seringapatam on May 15, Colonel Harris was in command of the second line. Cornwallis now fell back to Bangalore and prepared for the final advance.

Medows commanded the storming-party at the capture of Nandi

Drug on October 19. On this occasion, just as the stormers were about to move off to the attack, an officer was foolish enough to remark in the hearing of the men that there was said to be a mine near the breach; but the general at once cried out: "A mine! If it be a mine, my boys, it must be a mine of gold."

In the great attack on Tipu's fortified camp at Seringapatam during the night of February 6-7, 1792, General Medows was in command of the right column, which was intended to enter the camp and then turn to the left, so as to avoid the Eadgah Redoubt, and effect a junction with the centre under Cornwallis.

Medows was ordered to move in the centre of his column, and, owing to gross carelessness on the part of the staff officer concerned, the officer leading the advance of the column received written orders to turn to the *right* on entering the camp, instead of to the *left*. This brought the column up against the Eadgah Redoubt, which was only taken with heavy loss.

Medows left a detachment to hold the redoubt, and with the remainder of his column endeavoured to get into touch with Cornwallis.

The firing suddenly stopped; Medows could not tell whether the attack had succeeded or failed, and there was nothing to tell him where the other troops were. He was heard to exclaim:

Good God! I would at this moment give £10,000 of my fortune to know where Lord Cornwallis is.

The right column unwittingly passed within 400 yards of the centre under Cornwallis and reached Karigat Hill; and it was only a little before dawn—at 4 a.m. on the 7th—that the junction was effected.

Medows was in no way to blame for this affair, which was entirely due to bad staff work, but he took the failure terribly to heart. During the remainder of the operations he exposed himself recklessly and courted death. On one occasion, when he insisted on standing up on top of a parapet in full view of the enemy, Colonel Harris jumped up beside him, and said: "If you, sir, think it right to remain here, it is my duty to stand by you." The general then came down.

On February 23 hostilities ceased, and three days later General Medows, having failed to meet death at the hands of the enemy, deliberately shot himself. Fortunately, the wound did not prove fatal. An officer, who was going home on leave soon after, asked whether he could take any message to Mrs. Medows, and the general said:

Tell her that General Medows and Mr. Medows have settled their differences like gentlemen, and are now very good
friends.

During the first year of the war Medows did not prove himself a
great general, but he was always a very gallant officer and most popular with his troops. His supersession did not embitter him, and he supported Cornwallis most loyally. When the prize-money was distributed, both Cornwallis and Medows gave their shares to the men—in
the case of Medows this amounted to £11,000.

In August, 1792, Medows and Harris left Madras for England, and
Harris handed over to the general the sum of £40,000, which he had
saved from his pay and allowances during the four years in which he
had managed his affairs. When asked by his friends how he had managed to save so much General Medows replied: "Harris knows how he
scraped it together, but I don't."

This proved to be the last campaign in which General Medows
took part. He was made a K.B. in December, 1792, and promoted
lieutenant-general in October of the following year.

In January, 1798, he was promoted general, and he was commander-in-chief in Ireland for a short time in 1801.

Colonel Harris spent the year 1793 at home with his family, and
in 1794 he embarked for India with his wife and eldest daughter. He
joined the 76th Regiment at Calcutta in October—the very month
in which he was promoted major-general.

He was made commandant of Fort William, and remained for
more than two years at Calcutta. It was not till January, 1797, that
he learnt that in the previous May he had been given the local rank
of lieutenant-general, and appointed to the command of the Madras
Army. He reached Madras and assumed the command in February,
1797, and exactly a year later he found himself officiating as governor
of Madras. In May Lord Mornington reached Madras as governor-
general of India, and events now moved quickly towards another war
with Mysore.

Many of the chief civilian officials were very much afraid of Tipu,
but General Harris loyally and enthusiastically supported the governor-general, not only in his policy of making a firm stand against
Tipu, but even to the extent of weakening his own forces by detach-
ing troops to disband the French force at Hyderabad—a successful
enterprise which had the most far-reaching results.

In August, 1798, Lord Clive arrived and took over the duties of governor, thus leaving General Harris free to devote all his energies to his military duties.

The governor-general himself came to Madras in December. Harris had urged the advisability of the army being under the command of Sir Alured Clarke, the commander-in-chief in India; but Lord Mornington told him to consider well before he declined so great a command, and to give his answer next morning. Needless to say, he did not decline.

On February 11, 1797, General Harris left Vellore with an army of 20,000 men. He was joined by the Hyderabad contingent (16,000 strong) on March 9, at Kellamangalam.

The army was in sight of Bangalore on March 14, and reached Malvalli on the 27th. At Malvalli the first battle of the campaign was fought. Tipu was defeated, with the loss of 1,000 men killed and wounded, while the casualties of the victors only amounted to 63 killed and wounded, of which number 40 were Europeans.

General Harris decided to cross the Kaveri at Sosile to facilitate his junction with the Bombay Army of 6,000 men under General Stuart.

On April 4 the army was in position within a few miles of Seringapatam, and a month later, to the very day, the fortress was successfully stormed. During the siege operations the British casualties amounted to 67 officers, 835 Europeans, and 639 native soldiers killed, wounded, and missing.

General Harris announced his success in the following brief letter:

> To the Earl of Mornington.
>
> Seringapatam Camp,
> May 4, 1799.
>
> My Lord,
> I have the pleasure to announce to you that this day at one o'clock a division of the army under my command assaulted Seringapatam, and that at half-past two the place was entirely in our possession. Tippoo Sultaun fell in the assault. Two of his sons, the Sultaun Padshah and the Moize U'Deen, are prisoners with many of the principal *sirdars*. Our loss is trifling, and our success has been complete. I will forward to your Lordship details hereafter.

By the middle of August the whole of Mysore was in our possession and the country was pacified, so that General Harris was able to
hand over the command to Colonel Arthur Wellesley and return to
Madras to see the governor-general before his departure for Calcutta.
He described his journey down-country in the following letter to his
old chief, Sir William Medows:

> In seven months' absence from Madras, we not only took the
> capital of that enemy, who, you observe, should never have been
> left the power of being troublesome, but marched to the north-
> ern extent of his empire, and left it in so settled a state that I
> journeyed from the banks of the Toombudra 300 miles across in
> my *palankeen*, without a single soldier as escort, except, indeed,
> at many places the *polygars* and peons of the country, who in-
> sisted on being my guard through their respective districts. This
> was a kind of triumphal journey I did not dream of when set-
> ting off. The Almighty has been wonderfully bountiful to us. A
> conquest so complete in all its effects has seldom been known,
> and certainly in my respect left me nothing to ask.

In September Lord Mornington left Madras, but before doing so
he recommended General Harris most strongly for a Peerage of Great
Britain, and the Order of the Bath.

At the end of the year General Harris embarked for England. He
had already received the thanks of the House of Commons and of the
Court of Directors, and in February, 1800, he was appointed colonel
of the 73rd Highlanders; but so far from receiving any further honour
or reward, he found, when he got home, that the directors were strain-
ing every nerve to deprive him of the prize-money which had been
allotted to him by the governor-general. In December, 1804, General
Harris wrote an appeal to the Court of Directors, but it was not until
after six years of litigation and slander that these attacks were stopped,
and he was left in possession of his property.

Harris was promoted lieutenant-general in January, 1801, and general exactly eleven years later. He was not destined again to serve his
country in the field after his return from India, but it is interesting to
note that General Medows and he met once more in the course of
military duty.

After the disastrous ending of the expedition to Buenos Ayres in
July, 1807, General Whitelocke was tried by general court-martial and
cashiered after a trial lasting thirty-one days. Sir William Medows was

President of the Court, and among the other nineteen members there sat Lord Lake, Lieutenant-General Harris, and Sir John Moore. Sir William Medows died on November 14, 1813. at Bath, at the age of seventy-four

General Harris felt keenly the way in which his distinguished services had been ignored, and in January, 1815, he sent a memorial to the Duke of York, and a copy of the same to the Prime Minister. The result was that after the lapse of sixteen years he was at last, on August 11, 1815, raised to the peerage with the title of Baron Harris of Belmont in Kent, and of Seringapatam and Mysore in the East Indies.

In January, 1820, Lord Harris was made a G.C.B., and four years later he was appointed Governor of Dumbarton Castle. He died on May 19, 1829, full of years and honours.

He was not a brilliant commander, but he always proved himself a very gallant leader. In his younger days he was an admirable regimental officer, and when he first received an independent command, at the age of fifty-two, he loyally supported the governor-general in opposition to the timid counsels of the big-wigs of Madras; and he conducted the operations of the 1799 campaign with conspicuous success.

SIR WILLIAM MEDOWS.

Ensign, 50th Foot, February 26, 1757.

Lieutenant, 50th Foot, November 20, 1757.

Captain, 4th Horse, March 6, 1764.

Major, 4th Horse, October 1, 1766.

Lieutenant-Colonel, 5th Foot, December 31, 1769.

Lieutenant-Colonel, 12th Light Dragoons, September 17, 1773.

Lieutenant-Colonel, 55th Foot, September 22, 1775.

Lieutenant-Colonel, 5th Foot, October 7, 1777.

Colonel, November 25, 1778.

Major-General, November 20, 1782.

Lieutenant-General, October 12, 1793.

General, January 1, 1798.

A.D.C., November 25, 1778.

Colonel, 89th Foot, November 15, 1780.

Colonel, 73rd Foot, August 11, 1786.

Colonel, 7th Dragoon Guards, November 2, 1796.

Local Major-General, January 17, 1781.

K.B., December 14, 1792.

Lieutenant-Governor of the Isle of Wight, 1798.

Governor of Hull.

LORD HARRIS.

Ensign, 5th Foot, July 30, 1762.

Lieutenant, 5th Foot, January 2, 1765.

Adjutant, 5th Foot, September 2, 1767, till March 13, 1772.

Captain, 5th Foot, July 25, 1771.

Major, 5th Foot, October 7, 1777.

Lieutenant-Colonel, 5th Foot, December 29, 1780.

Lieutenant-Colonel, 76th Foot, October 12, 1787.

Colonel, November 18, 1790.

Major-General, October 3, 1794.

Lieutenant-General, January 1, 1801.

General, January 1, 1812.

Colonel, 73rd Foot, February 14, 1800.

Local Lieutenant-General, May 3, 1796.

Raised to the Peerage, August 11, 1815.

G.C.B., January, 1820.

Governor of Dumbarton, February 5, 1824.

9

Hale

At the time of the recent South African War there was a commonly accepted notion that "regrettable incidents" were unknown in the British army in former days. A slight knowledge of the history of the American War, or a perusal of an official work entitled *British Minor Expeditions, 1746-1814*, would have shown the absurdity of this idea.

It was further stated that in "the good old days" officers never criticized their commanders. These letters would seem to show that human nature is very much what it was, and that the British subaltern has not altered to any great extent during the last hundred and forty years.

William John Hale, the son of Admiral Hale, was born at Charleston, South Carolina, in 1756. He was gazetted lieutenant in the 45th Regiment on March 2, 1776. The regiment had left Ireland in 1775 for Halifax, and formed part of the force which sailed from that port in June, 1776, under Sir William Howe, for the New York Campaign.

The grenadier company of the 45th (to which Lieutenant Hale belonged), together with those of the 15th, 17th, 35th, 38th, 40th, 42nd, 43rd, 44th, 52nd, and 57th, formed the 2nd battalion of Grenadiers which was commanded by Lieutenant-Colonel Monckton of the 45th.

The following letter from the admiral gives a brief account of the action at King's Bridge on October 20 and the subsequent operations which led to the capture of Fort Washington:

To Mr. Palmer from Admiral Hale, Father to W. Hale.

Exeter, 22nd of Dec., 1776.

My Dear Friend,

This morning I received yours, and the same post brought us a letter from William, with two dates, one the 30th of Oct., the other 9th of Nov., giving an account of the action at Kings Bridge; he says he writes it under his marquee, is in good health and spirits, the rebel camp on a hill opposite them within cannon shot, and that they dispossessed them of it on the 20th as well as of a very strong post in their front, which they abandoned after a slight resistance to a single British brigade, though they had between 6,000 and 7,000 in their works; they stood on a hill opposite to them expecting with the utmost impatience to be ordered to attack them, and says there was a time when they might have been employed with good success.

About 200 were on the brow with two pieces of cannon and saluted them as they advanced through the valley, but to no purpose, for no sooner had Capt. Davis (who commanded the train) fired three shots at them than they instantly fled. When they had gained the summit they cannonaded each other for about a quarter of an hour, during which time they only wounded two men in the next file to him. though very few of their shots failed, as they could plainly distinguish the balls falling in the middle column and making dreadful havoc in it.

One of the rebel officers who was on horseback they saw cut in two; their hill being greatly superior to ours in height, made their shot go far beyond them; he says our artillery was admirably served under the control of Captain Davis. They dined together very heartily during the fire, but lay on their arms all night. The rebels gave out that they intended making a stand at that place, he says might have done it had they any spirit. Surely he says no men influenced by the like principles [illegible] in such a manner. He says our loss was very inconsiderable.

Col. Carr of the 35th, Capt. Gore of the 49th, Capt. Dearing of the 28th, died of their wounds, two were killed on the spot and a few wounded, among whom was Capt. Massey of the 35th (he names him because we knew him) who received a buck shot in the arm; about 70 privates killed and wounded. He saw about 30 or 40 of their dead the next morning, and 70 or 80 wounded, besides, as he was informed, 50 or 60 in the woods. 9th of Nov. he says since he wrote the above they had shifted their ground and was gone up the North River opposite the Jersies, to cut off the communication of the rebels with Fort Washington, besieged by Knyphausen.

The rebels abandoned four forts containing 72 pieces of cannon, to Phipps, Knyphausen's *aide-de-camp*, and three dragoons, this he says "they call a gallant defence!" They possess a strong chain of posts, and seem willing to draw our forces from one hill to another into the inner parts of the country, which would answer no end to us. After the surrender of that fortress it is supposed they will go into winter quarters. He begs I will acquaint his friends that they must look upon his letter to me as a letter to all. He begs I will send him the maps of that country last published, and a perspective glass, which I beg you will get that I may send him by the first opportunity.

My dear friend most affect.

J. Hale.

Admiral Hale,
Exeter,
Dec. 22nd, 1776.

Lieutenant Hale describes the pursuit to the Delaware and the capture of General Lee in the following letter:

Brunswick, New Jersey,
Dec. 19th, 1776.

We, the first and 2nd Battalions of grenadiers, are quartered here for the winter, as is generally believed, after having pushed the rebel vagabonds across the Delawar, and so intire possession of this province; we marched four days after them, but they outran our light infantry, indeed they seem to have forgotten everything but running. We pursued them to a ferry and found the boats burnt or carried off, which was no small disappointment as it was a forced march of 14 miles all night, and we had but six hours halt during the three preceeding days. A body of about 100 appeared on the opposite banks, but no firing past. We retired (after refreshing ourselves for an hour) the same evening to a little valley called Pennington, 15 miles distant, not a little fatigued.

A longer stay at this place was necessary, numbers of the men wanting shoes, having marched great part of the way barefoot; yet so eager was their desire of overtaking the flying enemy, that not a single complaint was uttered. While we remained here, we were agreeably surprised with the company of Mr. Lee, who was taken at a place called Basking-ridge, not far from Morris town, by 30 dragoons under Lt-Col. Harcourt; so great was his astonishment that for some time he would not believe himself a prisoner. I have visited him several times, though dejected he is very intertaining and communicative, asserting the Americans to be the best troops in the world, but says they are not in luck at present; he praises himself much on the affair in Carolina.

In a word he is the most sensible fool I know, anxious about his fate he is constantly enquiring what Gen. How intends, no one can resolve him, but as the gen. refused to see him, and threw his letter into the fire, many imagine that he is reserved for a general court-martial, if so, nothing can save him; he is very closely guarded, an officer remaining constantly in the same room. Sullivan commands his army till Gates arrives, but I believe that great officer will send no troops. How exclaimed when he was informed of it, that 'the War was ended.' Lee expected to be exchanged as Stirling and Sullivan were, his value however is too well known. The Congress and people speak of Washington's conduct with the greatest contempt, and Lee, if not the nominal commander-in-chief, would have had the sole direction of the active scenes of the next campaign.

A report that 16,000 men were determined to rescue him. General Grant, who at present commands in the Jerseys, will not permit any of us to go to York, in consequence of which I have neither bed or baggage; my clothes are all on my back and I am often obliged to wrap my cloak and blanket round me while I get my rags mended; we have no butter, wine or vegetables, though a market is promised.

A room is allotted me in this town, with only three doors in it, papered and well furnished, eight mahogany chairs, the bottoms compose my bed, a book-case and tables are the principal ornaments. Lord Cornwallis and General Vaughan are gone to England, the latter very obligingly sent me your letter; as soon as it arrived I delivered mine to him, but have not had an opportunity of seeing him since. I am not yet without hopes that when the Delawar freezes we shall see Philadelphia this season. The rebels crossed the Delawar at Trenton, whither they were pursued by the light infantry, Hessians, *grenadiers, and chasseurs,* who took some of them; as soon as they reached the other side they opened a battery of ten pieces of heavy cannon and, finding themselves safe, fired most furiously for some time, but only wounded two of the light infantry and one of the artillery. They boasted of an intended stand at this place; in our march from Fort Lee a few cannon balls, however, showed them the necessity of decamping, leaving behind a large quantity of stores, among them 11 pipes of Madeira which were distributed to the troops, each officer had a gallon. They halted at Princetown 17 miles from this, but on our approach fled to Trenton, some of their sculking parties yet infest the roads about New Bridge, if any taken no mercy will be used.

The campaign has been expensive, but to convince you that I am in no want of money, I enclose some bills which I desire you will accept and distribute to such of my friends as I would give them if in England. I am sensible how many letters I owe, but when I explain my finances it will not appear strange that I write only this, I am at present possessed of two sheets of paper besides this, they must be appropriated to the reports of my guard (I am now writing in the Barrack Guard Room); this ink such as it is comes from Capt. Phillips (Mrs. Gates' Brother), and if by the assistance of water I can subscribe my name it will be enough, but where wafers are to be procured is beyond my comprehension, nothing of the kind in the town.

Davis is quartered in Princetown, the prettiest situation in the Jerseys, I saw him three days since quite well, I intend visiting him soon, but as captains only are allowed to keep horses, I have bought an ass on which I propose travelling. Simcoe is with me, happiness indeed.

Your ever dutiful and affect.

W. Hale.

A month later he reports the "regrettable incident" at Trenton, and the stubbornly contested little action of January 3, 1777:

Brunswick, 15th Jan., 1777.

When I wrote you last, a body of Hessians was stationed at Trenton on the banks of the Delawar; through some fatal inattention they were surprised by the greatest part of the rebel army, who crossed the river above the town, while the remainder made a feint below to draw off Count Donnop, which succeeded. I was then at York with several officers of the Reserve to whom leave had been given on the supposition that we were perfectly safe from all incursions of fugitives, who had

164

abandoned the country with such precipitation. The day wet and stormy favoured their enterprise; Rall, advertised by Gen. Grant of this danger, had remained under arms during the night, but at the approach of day, imagining himself secure, returned to his quarters, which he had scarcely entered when the rebels poured into the town in columns, and killed or took prisoner the whole brigade, among the former was Rall, happy that his death left not on his misconduct the stain of treachery, which the proud spirits of Englishmen might have affixed to it.

I should have mentioned that about 400 made their escape. This intelligence made us all hasten to Brunswick where we left our troops, but found they had marched to Trenton, of which the rebels were in possession. We followed the next day with an escort of drafts and recruits for the grenadiers and light infantry. Between Brunswick and Princetown, we halted for some refreshments, and suffered the escort to go on before, but followed soon. Poor Captain Phillips (Mrs. Gates's brother) being better mounted was several yards in our front, and received a fire from some skulking peasants which mortally wounded him.

We pushed on, when 30 or 40 shots were made at us, but without hurting a man. I had just begun to contract an intimacy with him, whose character as an officer was equalled by few of his rank in the line, as a man surpassed by none; out of the pittance of a Lieut.'s pay he constantly allowed his Mother £20 a year; by his death she is again left destitute unless the generous humanity of an Howe recommends her to His Majesty. He lingered about 3 hours, often exclaiming, 'my poor Mother,' 'that unfortunate woman'; he gave me his campaign knife and some other trifles before he expired; one of the villains who mortally wounded a servant of Charles Mackenzie (Capt. Mackenzie's son, who with his brother George was taken the next day at Princetown where we left him sick) fell into our hands, I was strongly for hanging him pursuant to a general order for the treatment of such miscreants, but Capt. Williams of the 52nd opposed it; these belong not to their army, but fire on single officers for the sake of booty.

The next morning we left Princetown with the 17th, and 55th, a troop of mounted and other dismounted dragoons, the 40th remaining in the college at Princetown. About a mile and a half from that place we discovered the rebel army in two columns, entering a wood on the other side of a rivulet we had just passed. They had been driven out of part of Trenton the preceding day, but having broken down the bridge over a creek of the Delawar, which runs through the town, our troops could not pursue them that night, of which they took the advantage and filed off to attack Brunswick and Princetown imagined defenceless. We drew up on a woody eminence and looked at them for a considerable time, during which Col. Mawhood had two choices, either to retire back to Princetown, where with the other brigade we might have defended the works about it, or push on to Maidenhead where the 2nd Brigade lay; we suffered them however to extend their right between us and Princetown, we sent off the 55th to alarm the 40th, and then marched down with 330 to attack 8000 drawn up in regular order, and strongly posted in an orchard covered with some Barns.

The advanced guard of 800 reserved their fire till we advanced within 40 yards, and then gave us a very heavy discharge, which brought down 7 of my platoon at once, the rest, being recruits, gave way. I rallied them with some difficulty, and brought them on with bayonets, the rebels poured in a second fire, and killed Capt. Williams of the 52nd Grenadiers and Leslie of the 17th which regiment advanced in a most excellent order, and at length we drove them through the railings, barns and orchards, back on their main body which also fell into confusion, and I am convinced that had the other brigade been with us, we might have defeated the whole army.

We kept possession of the orchard for 20 minutes, turning one of their own guns upon them; during this time they discovered our weakness, and brought three pieces of cannon in play on our right with grape and case, but our nearness, 100 yards, saved us greatly. I now expected their flanks would wheel in and attack our rear, which had they done every man must have been cut to pieces. Our whole force was reduced to 240 when a resolution was taken to retreat, *i.e.,* run away as fast as we could; our loss is about 100, 15 out of 30 grenadiers and a captain, I was shot through my coat, and received a contusion on the leg, but am now very well and able to walk. We went 20 miles round that day to join our troops and marched all the following night to Brunswick, in all upwards of 40 miles without halting two hours; our quarters are now contracted and bad enough in reason, but we may live in them. God bless you,

believe me your ever affect.

W. Hale.

A letter written nearly five months later records the safe arrival of the "perspective glass," and one gathers that General Grant was not popular.

Brunswick, 6th June, 1777.

Hon. Sir And Madam.

Box, letters, and all came safe three or four days since, two of them have no date, but the 3rd which arrived first, is of the 23rd of March, and I imagine brought by the 'Carysford.' I wished to have found some tea in the box, which would have been a most acceptable present, only the coarsest *bohea* being sold at York, except a small quantity which was bought up at 8 dollars a pound; the glass an excellent one. I have had a ring fixed to it, and as it is far from heavy, I shall carry it on my back during the campaign, which we are just going to begin.

A large number of transports are taken up for the grenadiers and light infantry. S. Carolina is believed by many to be the place of our destination, though I cannot say that I am of that opinion. There are several forts up the N. River, some of strength, all of importance, as commanding the navigation of it, which are too high for the men of war to reach, at any rate, I hope we shall not be condemned to broil in that cursed climate for any considerable time, though my native place, I never wish to see it again.

I am as well pleased as you can be at my slight hurt at Princetown, for with all my enthusiasm I have not the least quarrel with a whole skin, and shall think myself obliged to the rebels for entertaining the same sentiments. As for news nothing material has happened since my last, except a descent in Connecticut under Sir William Erskine, where we destroyed at Danbury the grand magazine of their Northern army. Provisions enough to subsist 10,000 for 6 months, medicines, 1500 tents, arms, clothing, ammunition, flower, rum, etc., before this we destroyed at Peck's Hill a quantity of rum, pork, flour etc; in the Danbury affair our troops had a smart action with Arnold and Wooster and a large body of the rebels, whom the troops charged with bayonets. Wooster was mortally wounded.

God bless you, believe me most affect.

W. Hale,

Today we hang a spy.

General Grant's horse was killed under him by a cannon ball a few days since, as we were endeavouring to discover where the rebels entended going after striking their tents at Bound Brooke. I wish it had been the general instead of the horse, no man can be more detested.

The voyage to the Chesapeake and the landing of Howe's army for the Pennsylvania Campaign is described as follows:

Head of Elk River, Maryland,

30th August, 1777.

The last letter I had the pleasure of writing my dearest parents was dated off Staten Island; we imagined the Delawar our place of destination, but after appearing off that river, which some of the men of war went up, we bore away for Chesapeak Bay, and in five weeks from losing sight of the capes at last reached it. Happy it is for me that I do not sail in the navy, where I remember to have heard of a custom of throwing those passengers overboard whose sins and transgressions occasion contrary winds. I am certainly one of those unlucky beings, sixteen weeks from England to New York and my last voyage would sufficiently point me out as a proper sacrifice.

Though long, it was on the whole an agreeable passage, the weather fine, and not many thunder gusts. Col. Monckton and Major Gardiner (the genl's *aide de-camp*, now acting as major to our battalion) and a set of pleasing officers, made us bare the horrors of a ship with resignation the utmost to be expected. Our fresh provisions were indeed exhausted for more than three weeks before our landing, which was effected in flat boats, after a tedious rowing of six hours. The country was desolate of inhabitants, the men called to strengthen Washington, the women fled to avoid barbarities, which they imagined must be the natural attendants of a British army.

We passed three most uncomfortable nights in *wigwams*, drenched to the skin by those torrents of rain common in this southern climate; after refreshing the horses we marched to this place where 1500 men were assembled to protect a large quantity of stores. They had taken post on a steep hill surrounded by woods without the town, but on the light infantry and grenadiers preparing to attack them, they ran away without firing a shot. We found a great part of the stores remaining in the town, though they had employed several of the preceding days in removing them to Wilmington. 100 butts of Porter were left in one cellar, Madeira, rum, melasses, tobaco, yams, flour, etc; a number of sloops loaded with shoes, stockings, and rum, which had not time to escape, fell into our hands; we are now encamped, or more properly speaking enwigwamed, on the other side of the town, though our tents are now come up which is all we are allowed to carry.

By good fortune my canteen was brought this morning, for this week past we have lived like beasts, no plates, no dishes, no table cloth, biscuits supply the place of the first but for the others no substitute can be found; my clothes have not been off since we landed, and as the valice is left behind have no other prospect for sometime, however, clean straw is as good a bed as I desire, and if it does not rain am happy. A small quantity of port was brought on shore from some of the ships and sold before I knew it at three guineas a dozen. I have had only two fresh meals since quitting the ship, but the pork is so good as well for breakfast as dinner, that I feel no want of beef or mutton and was never in better health and spirits in my life. So much for household affairs, in which by the way I am a most capital manager.

Washington, on our leaving the Jersies, imagined we were going up the N. River to facilitate the progress of General Burgoyne, and crossed that river, but our appearing off the Delawar he returned and fortified himself at Newcastle on our leaving it. The wind being equally fair for New York or New England suspecting that we intended landing again on the Jersies, passed the Delawar and took possession of his old quarters at Morristown; finding at last that the fleet had entered Chesapeak Bay, he repassed the Delawar and is now at Wilmington 23 miles from this with only 8000 men, and gives out that he will make a stand there, which I very much doubt, for if we get on the other side of Brandy Wine Creek he must either break down the bridge over it which will cut off his retreat that way, or engage us, while another column marches below Wilmington

169

and hems in on that side; a few days will show what his intentions are. He must certainly be much perplexed, his situation is infinitely more delicate than it has yet been, if he leaves the inhabitated country, which unless he beats us he must do.

My friends will not expect to hear from me by this packet, when you inform them that I have borrowed this sheet, and that the ship sails tomorrow. I write this under a tree, while my black is making a fire to boil my pork, and my white servant pitching my tent.

My passage cost me but four guineas and half, though we drank claret all the way, every officer contributing so many days' pay made the expense very easy to the subalterns, and Col. Monckton supplied us with his own claret when ours was out. I have now said all I can except that I am

Your most affect.

Son

W. Hale.

The Battle of Brandywine took place on September 11, and is dealt with in a letter written about six weeks later:

Camp at Philadelphia
21st Oct., 1777.

The letter I wrote my dearest parents from the head of the Elk River dated the latter end of Aug. has I hope reached England long ere this. A single battle has since put us in possession of the capital of America, and deprived the rebels of their greatest source both of manufactures and commerce. On our march towards the Schuylkil we had several skirmishes with their scouting and advanced parties, none of them considerable enough to deserve mentioning except one at Iron Hill where 1500 of them, consisting of volunteers and riflemen, defended a brook with steep woody banks which we must pass. The light infantry, however, soon drove them, and the army proceeded on its march to Philadelphia.

Sensible of the importance of that city, they had cautiously avoided an engagement till that alone could save it. The principle ford over the Brandywine Creek was commanded by a strong height, on which they had thrown up a redoubt defended by their left wing under General Maxwell. On the morning of the 11th we moved in two columns towards the creek;

the right under Gen. Knyphausen passed the ford and carried the redoubt with the trifling loss of about twenty killed and wounded; in it were found three pieces of cannon and an howitzer.

The left column under Gen. How being obliged to follow the winding of the creek, after a march of 17 miles and crossing it twice, came in sight of the rebels drawn up in four lines on very advantageous ground behind railings about five o'clock. We immediately formed, and began the attack, the grenadiers charged and drove them from six successive railings under an exceeding heavy fire, while the light infantry drove a much superior body out of a wood on our left, a column moving to attack the left of our battalion were engaged by part of the 4th brigade and routed.

The action continued till dark, which alone saved their whole army from total destruction, as our right was marching towards us after putting their left to the route; the battle continued for three miles, and we took up our ground on the place where it ended. Nothing could be more dreadfully pleasing than the line moving on to the attack; the grenadiers put on their caps and struck up their march, believe me I would not exchange those three minutes of rapture to avoid ten thousand times the danger. Our loss, the 2nd Grenadiers, does not exceed 83 killed and wounded, that of the rebels about 700, but the desertions made the whole full 6000, and 13 pieces of cannon.

Ten days after this Gen. Gray with his brigade and the 2nd Light Infantry surprised a rebel brigade of 1500 under General Wayne, of whom he killed between 3 and 400; the darkness of the night favoured the attempt, which was executed with the greatest silence, not a shot being fired on our side. As our light infantry gave no quarter very few prisoners were taken. On the 25th the British and Hessian grenadiers took possession of this place, and the next day the *Delawar* frigate of 28 guns which fired upon the town to prevent us from raising any works, was obliged after running aground to strike to two six-pounders.

The 4th of Oct. the whole rebel army under cover of a fog attacked the outposts of the army at Germantown and obliged the light infantry who engaged them for near two hours to give way; but being quickly supported by the brigades, they were repulsed, and our battalion, which marched from Philadelphia to their assistance, pursued them eight miles, but were only able to get near enough to exchange a few cannon shot with them. Sir H. Clinton has taken the forts up the N. River which were exceedingly strong by storm. In them were found near 100 pieces of cannon, the 57th were there, but James was not touched in the affair at Germantown.

I mentioned that the river was not cleared of the *chevaux de fraise* and I fear it will take sometime. Mud Island is in their possession, where they have a strong fort defended by row gallies and floating battery and several ships; in the only passage where no cassines were laid they had sunk three hulks. On the Jersey shore, at a place called Red Bank, is another very strong fortification which commands the island and protects both that and their shipping.

Four days since the Hessian Grenadiers attempted to carry it by storm, but after getting over their outworks they found a wet ditch between them and the inside fort, and being flanked by the gallies, who kept up a most tirable fire, on one side and a bastion on the other, they were obliged to retreat with a considerable loss. Col. Donnop was wounded and taken. The *Augusta, Roebuck, Pearl* and *Mirlin* at the same time endeavoured to get up to the Island, but found the *chevaux de fraise* impassable. The *Augusta* struck and was obliged to be burnt after the people were taken out, and the *Mirlin* who covered them shared the same fate. Red Bank, I hear, is to be regularly invested.

Mr. Craig has shown me every civility in his power, and wants me much to live at his house, which I cannot possibly do on account of the distance from the camp, though a tent begins to feel rather cold, and I have no other covering than my cloak, the remainder of my baggage being on board, so that I am almost as ragged as last year. Tea is almost unknown. here, and nothing can be more acceptable than a few pounds.

Your most dutiful and affectionate

W. Hale.

We learn that the cost of living at Philadelphia was very high from a letter dated January 20, 1778:

The uncommon mildness of the season having kept the river open affords an opportunity of which I had indeed despaired of acquainting my dearest parents that I am still alive and in as good health as ever. Nothing material has happened lately; the taking Mud Island and Red Bank; the glorious fall of the gallant Dunop and the loss of the *Augusta* etc. have been already detailed to you from better authority and material than I can possibly give them.

We have indeed marched out with a view of bringing Washington to an action which he continuously declined, and as he was too strongly entrenched to admit our forcing his lines under the loss of two thousand men, much too great a price at this advanced season, we returned with several prisoners among whom was a Brig. Gen. Irvine, a hatter of this place; before taken in Canada and dismissed upon parole, which nevertheless is again accepted as a proper security, a mode of carrying on the war which we seem lately to have adopted with proportionable success. Possibly the loss of three fingers which will incapacitate him from following his trade may have been the humane inducement to so particular indulgence; this, and a few foraging parties, constitute the whole of our military transactions since the departure of the last packet.

I am extremely concerned at being obliged to inform you that I have not received a single article of my baggage, excepting my bedstead from the regt. Whether taken, driven to the West Indies, or not sent is impossible for me to say, the want of it, however, reduced me to the same distress as if totally lost: six shirts were my campaign stock, and by unavoidable bad usage they are now barely serviceable for lint. My jacket (an old coat turned) cannot now be resembled to any earthly clothing; transparent as that of the in-habitants of light.

In this distress I have been forced to borrow from Bellew the sum of twenty guineas, which with my pay have barely sufficed, to get me a suit of clothes and six shirts. Could you form an idea of the misery of the army you would envy a common sailor. My epaulets cost a guinea and a half each, my linen, 6/- the exclusive making, scarlet cloth six dollars, white 25/-sterl. Had this additional burthen been incured by any vice, by any expensive folly, my heart could not thus distress your feelings.

Let me add the enormous price of every article of life; meat for a considerable time before the taking Mud Island 3s/6d currency a pound, common brown sugar a dollar; from this Great Britain may judge of the vast sums lavished on commissaries, quarter masters etc. and the consequent distress of those whose blood and toils are held as nothing in the parliamentary scale of supplies.

Such is my present situation with regard to promotion; all vacancies in the flank companies are filled up from the battalion in which they happen. Ours has been a lucky corps, that is, they have lost but few captains, one was killed at Brandywine and his comp. fell to the lot of an old lieut. who. indeed, had been 19 years in the army, but had never been within reach of a shot, from lameness that day, in his life. On the contrary a most excellent officer—an acquaintance of my Uncle Graham's, Peebles, after being fourteen years in the grenadier company, shot through the body in Bouquet's affair with the Indians, has after 23 years service attained the rank of Capt. Lt. Such is the lottery of a military life, whatever my chance may be I shall still adhere to my original principle; that the duty to a parent state is or ought to be, the ruling system of every man.

my dear parents' most dutiful and affect.

W. Hale.

Two months later Lieutenant Hale wrote the following long letter. It is amusing to note that articles like tea and cloth were very liable to go astray on the lines of communication. A similar phenomenon was often observed in South Africa in the case of parcels containing tobacco.

Philadelphia, 23rd March, 1778.

Nothing could give me greater pleasure after so long silence than the receipt of your three letters, Oct., Nov. and Dec. all agreeing in the most pleasant account of your health and situation. I had almost despaired of hearing from Europe till spring, but the river opened much earlier than was expected, indeed, the winter has been remarkably mild, though from snow and rain by no means as pleasant as the last.

I find by your latest letter that the news of Burgoyne's misfortune had reached England, when I doubt not a great firment was raised, though the affair of Bennington must in some measure have prepared the minds of the people for such an event. He had long expected it from the accounts in the rebel papers of the militia etc. collecting at places in his rear and effectually cutting off all possibility of retreating to Ticonderoga, embarassed with so large a train of heavy artillery, destitute of intelligence or guides, in a country perhaps by nature one of the strongest in the world, perpetually harassed by forces acquainted with every defile through which he must necessarily pass, and headed by the most enterprising and active gen. in the rebel service, for such Arnold undoubtedly is, Gates being chiefly employed in hanging Tories at Albany.

Add to this the infamous behaviour of the Brunswickers who could never be prevailed on to face the enemy, and it will by no means appear surprising that a gen. thus circumstanced should fail in his designs; but while I am satisfied that Burgoyne has done everything in his power to fulfil his orders, I cannot help commenting the general delusion that seems to have prevailed in England of Philadelphia's being the principle object, and that in consequence of our possessing it, the submission of all America would necessarily follow. The direct contrary is the truth, by co-operating with the Northern Army, the reduction of New England would in all human probability have been ensured, and had Washington been disposed to assist them the long march through the Jersies at that season would have been attended with very bad effects to his army.

From Burgoyne's letter it is clear that he acted in conformity to his orders from home; and Gen. How pleads the same excuse for marching to this place, which militated so strongly against his inclination and opinion that I am told from very good authority, he has sollicited his recall. Numberless reasons pointed out the New England colonies as objects infinitely superior to this province. The *Liverpool, Pearl* and *Camilla* blocked up their fleet of ships and gallies in the Delawar and the *Lizard* alone guarded the harbour of Charlestown. I need not inform you that the infinity of creeks and harbours along the northern coasts would baffle all the efforts of the whole English Navy; from these the rebels are supplied with every article which the kindness of the French and Dutch send them.

Nor when in consequence of the fatal instructions Philadelphia was fixed upon, was our method of carrying the plan into execution the most faultless. In our appearance off the capes of Delawar, the *Roebuck* came out, and Capt. Hammond going on board the admiral produced a Chimerical draught of fortifications that were never erected and *chevaux de frise* that were never sunk. This intelligence caused us to bear away for the Chesapeak, which calms and contrary winds prevented us from reaching till another month had elapsed; instead of which had we landed at Newcastle, 40 miles only below this, Philadelphia must have fallen into our hands, and we been at liberty to pursue the routed army as far as we pleased.

Six weeks too, of the finest campaign weather were suffered to slip away in a most shameful inactivity till the rebels had not only recovered from the panic of Brandywine, but become daring enough to attack our advanced post at German-town. This time employed in forming magazines of forage, would have saved us considerable trouble at this season, as we were obliged often to go out 18 or 20 miles to collect hay. The light infantry are just returned from the Jersies, where they were sent in order to cut off a convoy under Gen. Wayne, who had the start of them; however they took a few waggons loaded with a mixture called by the rebels, rum, but procured no forage.

These foraging parties are very peaceable, quite different from our Jersey excursions last year, when we were generally sure of fighting twice a week. The rebels have refused to let Burgoyne and his troops go home agreeable to the terms of the convention, until it shall be ratified by the Parliament, a measure, says the resolution of Congress, rendered absolutely necessary by the perfidy of the British Nation and its generals, hoping [by] this violation of public faith to make us treat with them on the footing of independent states.

Enough of this disagreeable subject. I do not believe I have once mentioned my opinion of Philadelphia, which so far from admiring, that I would not exchange a dungeon in New York for the governor's house in this city. The situation, in a dead flat where there is nothing for many miles to relieve the eye, is in itself sufficient to disgust any but a native of the place, who has never seen another; a most disagreeable sameness reigns throughout the streets in which there is not a single public building to attract the notice or attention of an European, the State House is a mean, and at the same time heavy, piece of architecture; nor have the hospital and bettering house any other claim to merit, than what their utility allow, but agreeably to the levelling principles of the Quakers, a man no sooner builds a good house, than three or four dirty hovels are run up close to him, that he may not forget the pristine equality.

Plainness and convenience were the only objects of the founders and to these their descendants have strictly adhered. For my own part, were I condemned to live in America I should prefer Staten Island to any part I have seen. I cannot help observing that all the plans of Philadelphia concur in representing the city as extending from the Delawar to the Schylkill, agreeable to the design of Mr. Penn, whereas in fact six streets only out of fourteen deserve that name, the rest consisting of scattered houses. Our amusements are assemblies and plays, each once a week; as I have never been or intend to be at either, I cannot give any account of them. My time is at present fully employed in learning the German language, which I find almost absolutely necessary for the frequency of British officers being detached with Hessians, a better opportunity of making a proficiency can never happen and I hope to master it, though the most disagreeable and difficult in pronunciation of any in Europe, the Russian excepted.

Rooms are opened at the city tavern by a subscription of two days' pay from each officer, a genteel coffee house where you meet and converse or play from six o'clock to twelve; to prevent any disorders an officer's guard from the grenadiers mounts there every evening, Sundays excepted, when the rooms are shut. Tea, coffee, lemonade and *Orgeat* are the only liquors allowed, except on ball nights, when Negus is permitted; the apartments are elegantly furnished and in one of them Capt. Wreeden of the Hessian *yagers* keeps a Pharaoh Bank which has not a little disordered the finances of several officers who have been imprudent enough to endeavour at carrying away two thousand guineas.

I am extremely sorry to say that the example of men high in rank seems to give a sanction to a vice so destructive to the Army, and so fatal to individuals. Prince Ferdinand encouraged play by his example, which appears to me astonishing. This army is now ten times worse officered than it was two years since, owing to that extravagant rage for play, which prevailed at York and Brunsick last year, and many officers, respectable for their experience in their profession as well as for their private characters, will be obliged to sell out before the troops take the field; their places must be filled by others who have no other merit than that of their money being lodged. Lansquenet and *vingt-un* have also a number of votaries; but dice have not yet been introduced. To the honour of Gen. Knyphausen I must add that he discourages by every means in his power this pernicious amusement.

I am much obliged to you for the tea you promise, but wish all things of that sort, or cloth could be sent by men-of-war directed to the regt. at York, who will forward them by good opportunities. Ours and the 35th are to remain here, to the great mortification of their respective flank companies who have all the danger and fatigues to themselves without the chance of raising by the fortune of war. The ensueing campaign will, it is thought, be a very active one. Washington in his late address to the militia earnestly intreats them to repair to him in such numbers as may enable him to act upon the offensive and strike a decisive blow; what effect this will have on them is uncertain, but deserters come in in great numbers every day all agreeing in the account of sickness, poverty and distress of every kind, reigning in their camp at the Great Valley Forge, the appearance of these miserable creatures sufficiently confirms the truth of their assertions, some without shoes or stockings, others in rags; and all exhibiting a picture of the most extreme wretchedness; to clothe their troops even in this manner, the most cruel and arbitrary measures are employed.

The people of the country are allowed only one suit of cloths each; the number of blankets to a family, nay even the women's petticoats of which they make coverlets, is limited, their only liquor is a kind of whiskie expressed from the stalk of Indian corn. The use of this was found so prejudicial to the men's health in the campaign before the last that it was prohibited. Of fresh provisions they feel as yet no want, though cattle are brought from the Jerseys, the country all round them being totally impoverished, during the space of thirty miles from Philadelphia not a man is to be seen in any of the villages or farm houses under sixty yean of age, all is solitary and desolate. Even in Virginia the greatest source of their best, their only serviceable troops, the price of a substitute in the militia is 600 continental dollars, and if he deserts or is rendered incapable of serving, another must be supplied perhaps at the same price and with the same difficulty.

The Act for obliging criminals to work on the Thames, has been felt in the most sensible manner by the rebels, their whole body of fighting men being principally composed of convicts, the remainder of indented servants, to whom these champions of liberty have intrusted their independance; the native Americans have never yet fought, and I am thoroughly satisfied never will. Some few Virginians and Marylanders excepted, they are the most dastardly wretches of the Almighty's creation.

The officers who served in this country during the last war declare them the same at present as when they dreaded an Indian in every thicket, a national character is hardly conquered nor have the rebels found the Declaration of Independance able to rouse their hypocrisy to defend their religion, or their avarice their property with manly courage; to increase their calamities the Indian tribes on the Ohio, exasperated at the death of the 'Great Corn-stalk,' a chief who signalized himself greatly in the Indian War of 1763, and was lately murdered at a talk by the rebels; as well as at the want of the customary presents, have tomahawked and scalped a great number of the inhabitants of the back settlements, who are flying to Fort Pitt for shelter; Gen. Hand with a large body of the militia and 8 pieces of cannon is marched against them.

Lord Chatham particularly honours us with his account of the present state of our army; undisciplined, disorderly, and daily growing worse and worse, is, it seems, our condition; deplorable circumstances, it must be confessed, and were not our enemies fortunately for us, rather worse situated in; these respects God knows the consequence, nor would his lordship believe the inhabitants of Philadelphia themselves, should they inform him that the city was never known to enjoy greater tranquillity in the time of the most profound peace or to be so free from disorders of every kind as at present.

That the markets are regularly supplied with provisions, at a much dearer rate it must be expected. Bread is the most extravagant article, a loaf of the same size as a two penny one in England costing two shillings currency, or 15/-sterling, but a quantity of flour is expected from New York, which will considerably lower the price. Butter, which is very good, is commonly sold at ½ a dollar a pound. Meat is generally from 7½d to 9d , poultry is by no means so cheap, fowls about 10/- currency, (6/3) a couple, but turkeys (very small) 3 dollars each. Liquors are reasonable and good, particularly Madiera.

To us who are accustomed to the extravagance and poverty of Brunswick, and to paying a dollar a pound for meat in this place before the river was opened, these prices appeal trifling, though terrible enough to freeze the blood of a whole circle of Devonshire housekeepers, who would be rather puzzled to discover how these expenses can be supported on 3/6 a day.

The matter is problematical undoubtedly, and but for living almost at no expense during the campaign refraining from gaming in winter, with the help of European friends, could not long be sustained, hope you have long since received my letter by Gov. Wentworth, in which I acquainted you of the loss or neglect of sending my baggage, which I know not. Till the return of Captain Ross from York, the present inconvenience was equal in either case; and with the dearness of provisions obliges me to have recourse to Bellew much more than wished or intended to have done, he will satisfy you that the money has been applied to no improper use, and of the situation of affairs at that time.

I should have been glad of a more circumstantial detail of publick recurrences than either of your letters give; by the papers I find more Germans are to be hired, would to God England could raise an equal number of men, the behaviour of the Brunswickers is too recent to be forgotten; and the Hessians, who are allowed to be the best of the German troops, are by no means equal to the British in any respect. I believe them steady, but their slowness is of the greatest disadvantage in a country almost covered with woods, and against an enemy whose chief qualification is agility in running from fence to fence and thence keeping up an irregular, but galling fire on troops who advance with the same pace as at their exercise.

Light infantry accustomed to fight from tree to tree, or charge even in woods; and grenadiers who after the first fire lose no time in loading again, but rush on, trusting entirely to that most decisive of weapons the bayonet; will ever be superior to any troops the rebels can ever bring against them. Such are the British, and such the method of fighting which has been attended with constant success. At Brandywine, when the line first formed, the Hessian grenadiers were close in our rear, and began beating their march at the same time with us; from that minute we saw them no more till the action was over, and only one man of them was wounded by a random shot which came over us.

The surprise at Trenton, and the repulse at Red Bank, where however they behaved very gallantly, have made the rebels entertain a very mean opinion of them, which may perhaps betray those gentlemen into a disagreeable situation, should they ever be engaged in ground that will allow the Hessians to display their skill in manoeuvring, they themselves make no scruple of owning our superiority over them, but palliate so mortifying a confession by saying 'Englishmen be the divel for going on, but Hesse men be soldier.' They will not readily fight without being supported by their cannon which we think an useless incumbrance. Gen. Knyphausen who is said to be one of the best generals in Germany, bred up under Marshal Keith to whom he was *aide de camp,* has by the severity of his discipline in a great measure put a stop to the infamous practice of plundering, which was much encouraged by De Heister who shared in the profits of this lucrative occupation.

I observe with great pleasure the credit given us by the general for our constancy in supporting the fatigues of the march from the head of the Elk River to Philadelphia; which were really great, our best habitations *wigwams,* through which the heavy rains of this climate whenever they fell easily penetrated, the season however proved so favourable as not to incommode us often in this manner. At our first landing the rain fell three nights successively, and we had only the cloths on our backs, the only resource was standing by a large fire next morning till they were dried not a very agreeable method in the heat of August Our rum too failed some days before the action and the quality of the different waters we were obliged to drink gave me the bloody flux, by which I was so weakened as to faint twice in the morning of the affair.

However I recovered strength sufficient to go through the fatigue of the afternoon, Col. Monckton supplied me with claret, in which I mixed *ipecacuanha* and rhubarb, a never failing medicine. Notwithstanding the lateness of the year when we returned from our excursion to Derby the 31st of Dec. where we went into winter quarters, till which time I constantly slept in my cloths from the first landing, I never enjoyed a greater share of health than at present.

With love to all believe me

Your most dutiful and affect.

W. Hale.

The following letter shows that the army now fully realized the serious nature of the task before it:

Philadelphia, 12th April, 1778.

Since the expedition to White Marsh, our life has been uniformly peaceable, the rebels indeed threatened to attack our Lines, in order to keep up the spirits of their people, by promising them the repossession of Philadelphia, though Washington never entertained the most distant idea of such an event. His whole force from the time of his going into winter quarters at the Great Valley Forge scarcely amounting to 6000 men, and ours consisting of nearly three times that number. At that place he has built a set of barracks entirely of wood by no means contemptible, his power being absolute, all the country people round him were compelled to contribute their assistance, by which means they were erected in a very short time. I know not in what manner they are fortified, but the whole ground is a natural fortification, a steep rocky hill for many miles, we were encamped on it during two days immediately before we past the Schuylkill in our march to Philadelphia.

In what part of the continent the operations of the ensuing campaign will commence, I am at a loss to conceive. Washington will never attempt to cover Pennsylvania; indeed it is so much exhausted as to be scarcely worth the trouble. Figure to yourself two large armies, the one flying from the other and both sweeping all before them, not only the present stock is destroyed, but all the young cattle, the future dependency of the province. Desolation triumphs all around; nor will a century repair the loss America has already sustained in population and commerce, burthened with debt beyond the ability of the most flourishing state in Europe to discharge.

The rebellion has cost her by disease and the sword upwards of 100,000 men. A person of this place had the curiosity to keep an exact account of the sums emitted at different times in continental money by the Congress; this estimate he lately published and to the best of my recollection, for I have not the paper immediately at hand, it amounts to the considerable sum of four million one hundred and twenty thousand pounds sterling. Their commerce is almost totally ruined, and what little specie yet remains among them must be sent to foreign nations for the purpose of prolonging a war every day of which plunges them still further in misery and ruin.

The leaders have gone too far to recede, and the people, having parted with the means of freeing themselves from the tyranny of their oppressors, are obliged to submit. Perhaps never was a rebellion so universal and intense as this; a circumstance which affords in my opinion a most convincing refutation of the patriotic assertion that America was forced into independance. No sudden commotion could have been prepared for, or sup-ported with such obstinacy, so unlooked-for a transition. A negotiation for an exchange of prisoners is just broken off by the rebels refusing to treat with Gen. How, but with the Parliament of Great Britain.

Believe me, my dear Sir, most sincerely yours

W. Hale.

P.S. Direct to me 45th Comp. 2nd Batt. Grenadiers in Sir W. Howe's Army."

A letter written only eight days later bears testimony to the popularity of Sir William Howe and the regret felt in the army at his departure.

Philadelphia, 20th April, 1778.

To the Turks, another barbarous nation, we owe the custom of punishing commanders for failing in their schemes and enterprises. To Britain the world is indebted for the extraordinary spectacle of a general punished, for succeeding in all he has ever undertaken. Ministers say they have been deceived by representations from this quarter of the readiness of the rebels to return to their allegiance, and that several had actually taken the oaths.

Excepting the equally false and ridiculous boast of Gov. Tryon, the ministry have not been deceived in this particular at least; during the whole of our progress through the Jersies, and every other part of the continent, innumerable crowds attended to take the oaths, and receive protection in return; if afterwards, not thinking themselves bound by the most solemn ties that can be imposed on human beings, they took up arms and watched every opportunity of employing them against us, is the general, who transmits a faithful account of these faults, or the people who set at naught the most sacred obligations, acceptable?

To enumerate the numbers taken in arms with protections in their pockets would be to transcribe the provost lists. I cannot however help mentioning that the man who shot Phillips, was of the number; America, I believe, will grant you the peace you so desire, however it may be the Interest of a few able bankrupts in the Congress, that the war should be prolonged in the same manner as at present.

Whether you can send a better gen. than Sir William How, I know not, one more beloved will with difficulty be found. From Lord North's speech I gather that if these proposals are rejected, America will be left to independence; should it be the case, England will sink beneath its primitive insignificance, and be un worth the regard of any state, or individual, who think honour to be reckoned among the goods of the world. For my own part I shall never wish to revisit it. Where-ever I may be cast I shall always remain your most dutiful and affect. son

W. Hale.

On May 9 he wrote as follows to his brother:

Sorry I am that it is not in my power to increase your importance by a packet of news—the great secret of becoming consequential in a country village. Had it not been for Gen. How's recall I should have been able to give you an account of the storming Washington's entrenchment at the Valley Forge, where his force is by no means of sufficient strength to preclude such an attempt, nor do I think it would have cost us more than two thousand men at the utmost, and the blow if followed must have effectually ruined the rebel army. Whether Gen. Clinton, who as commander in chief must be one of the commissioners of the late bill, will think himself tied up by that circumstance from acting offensively I know not, but am convinced of the practicability of the scheme.

Washington has sent away his heavy artillery, Twelve pounders are the largest guns left with him, which are too light for the defence of works, nor has he any magazines within his lines, the army depending for its subsistence on the supplies from Maryland and Virginia.

I sent the resolves of Congress relating to an accommodation with England by cannon, since which the transaction with France has appeared. War I doubt not is proclaimed long before this can reach you; it will be mostly naval, unless she chooses to send troops to this country.

The design of sending out commissioners will, I suppose, be laid aside; the alliance with France, as it must be founded on a misrepresentation of the situation of America, cannot prove of long continuance. The Congress have assured the French that they are in no want of troops, but that the great natural resource is almost exhausted, nor will they be able, militia and all included, to bring more than twelve thousand men into the field this campaign: imagination cannot figure to itself the depopulation which this country has undergone.

The 22nd Light Infantry are just returned from an expedition up the river, where they have burnt two fine frigates of 32 guns that lay at Burlington, called the *Effingham* and *Washington*, besides other vessels to the amount of 34 sail, their Gallies were scuttled and sunk on the first appearance of our boats and gallies; they have brought with them some pieces of cannon, and rendered several others unserviceable, the damage done the rebels is computed at 200,000, and it was effected without the loss of a man.

Dear John, most affect yours

W. Hale.

In the following letter, written just before the evacuation of Philadelphia, it is amusing to note that the writer has far more confidence in the military abilities of his own captain than in those of Cornwallis:

Philadelphia, 15th June, 1778.

Just before the departure of Gen. Howe we moved out to surprise the Marquis de la Fayette who was encamped with 2000 men on the banks of Schuylkill, not far from Whitemarsh; the surprise was so nearly accomplished that they forded the river with so great precipitation in small parties of ten or twelve men as to miss the ford and several were carried down the stream and drowned. Had this attempt succeeded the gen. entended to

185

have followed and attacked their lines. Gen. Grant, who commanded the light infantry and grenadiers, the advanced corps, is blamed for not securing the ford as the guide advised.

We marched from ten at night till eight in the morning at what is called the grenadier step without halting ten minutes, and after a tour of 47 miles returned that night to Philadelphia; some men died on the road from the heat and excessive fatigue. Having no horse I walked the whole way except the last five miles, when my strength being nearly exhausted I accepted a horse.

Since the receipt of yours of the 2nd April the commissioners have arrived, what success will attend their embassy is as yet uncertain. I do not think the Americans will give up independence, the great reward of fifteen years plots and struggles. The terms are I doubt not sufficiently humiliating on our side; one of their officers who came in the other day with a flag of truce told me that he believed the Congress, and the people, would have no objections to the proposals, but the alliance with France, which he said their honour would not suffer them to violate.

I could not help asking him whether the tender conscienced Americans regarded a breach of faith with so perfidious a nation as France as a crime of blacker dye than a violation of an oath of allegiance. That the body of the people are inclined to peace on the terms now offered them is certain; and of their aversion to the French a most remarkable instance has lately happened: the *Greyhound* frigate fell in with a French ship of 22 guns, and while the preparations were making for action, forty rebel prisoners petitioned Capt. Dickson to be quartered at the guns, which he granted, and after taking the Frenchman gave them a schooner and dismissed them with a guinea each; they have since entered into our navy, declaring they will never fight for France.

In what light her conduct is regarded by the other nations of Europe I know not, but it is the most flagrant act of atrocious perfidy recorded in the annals of any people. If we are to continue the war with America, I should very gladly attack their West India Settlements, so conveniently situated for a sudden stroke; every preparation is making for leaving this city, our horses and bat-men are this day gone into the Jersies where a body of troops under Gen. Lesslie have been for sometime encamped with all the waggons and provisions.

The heavy artillery are embarked, so that we shall move in all probability tomorrow or the day following; our march through the country, which by the shortest route is 45 miles, will not I believe meet with any considerable obstruction, some scattered firing on our flanks and rear must be expected. At York it is thought the flank corps will be dissolved, and the companies reunited to their respective regts. I fear I must descend, painful thought, from the awful sublimity of a grenadier to the plebeian state of a common battalion officer, not that I intend leaving the company which I at present command, Ross being appointed *aide de camp* to the wretched Cornwallis, who to the equal concern and astonishment of the thinking part of the army, all ready too well acquainted with his abilities, made his appearance with the commissioners.

You at home must certainly entertain a very different opinion of him from us, hurrying him away at only six days notice. The excellent understanding of Ross will, however, in great measure correct the defects of his lordship, whose respectable character in private life cannot fail of making us regret his being placed in a station to the duties of which he is so very unequal; at the head of a brigade his personal bravery would have entitled him to every commendation a quality so universal can demand. Situated as I am at present you will not be surprised at my wishing for a continuance or rather the opening a campaign, in the course of which I might at the head of a company of grenadiers hope to enforce the recommendation of my most valued friend Bellew.

My hardships which you deplore with such paternal fondness are not as great as the distance between us makes you imagine. The meanest soldier utters not a word of complaint at sharing them, why then should we? From your bounty I am enabled to leave this town unindebted, a circumstance not otherwise to be accounted for. Capt. Bellew has I doubt not acquainted you of our situation, meat seldom less than 2/-a pound, and every other article in the same proportion. My character, I am persuaded you are satisfied by men whose own are irreproachable, has ever been unstained by dissipation or debauchery; attached to my profession, from principle I have never risked my commission at a gaming table to support the unavoidable expenses of a bare subsistence; except one play, I went to no place of publick amusement; yet with the strictest economy I have been obliged more than once to anticipate my pay.

I shall give you a sketch of my management; two coats have constituted the whole of my wardrobe, my appearance till I was certain my baggage could not arrive, was such as to entitle me to a whipping in England as a vagabond, but here was not a very striking phenomenon. I purchased a coat which is now turned and made into a jacket for the campaign at present on my back; the cloth you sent me, arrived time enough to be worn about a dozen times, with the addition of another epaulet (2-15-0) and is now deposited in my chest. Had we taken the field I should be well enough pleased, but our stay at York will I fear oblige me to trespass still further on your goodness; can. I request £20? I am sensible of the injustice of it, but at the same time convinced that you would; not wish me to appear unworthy the character of your most dutiful and affect, son

W. Hale.

The 2nd Battalion of Grenadiers played a prominent part in the Battle of Monmouth Court House, and lost 98 officers and men killed and wounded. The total British casualties were only 380 (including 60 deaths from sunstroke). Lieutenant Hale describes the action thus:

Camp at Neversunk,
4th July, 1778.

The shortness of time must apologize to my dearest parents for the scanty portion of paper which informs them that I am perfectly in health at this place—the boundary of our march through the Jersies. Gen. Clinton's dispatches will acquaint you of an action on the 28th June, of which as our battalion bore the principal part you will expect some account. Lee, from whose former conversation I well knew acquainted with the temper of our present commander, laid a snare which perfectly succeeded. The hook was undisguised with a bait, but the impetuosity of Clinton swallowed it. A few light troops began a desultory kind of attack on the flank of our rear guard, composed of the grenadiers and light infantry and Rangers, in which the Rangers were chiefly engaged, and Simcoe received a flesh wound in the arm.

Larger bodies were then seen quitting the woods, and filing off towards some heights in our rear, passing within cannon shot of our battalion. Through my glass I plainly saw from their variegated cloths they did not belong to our army, but Col. Monckton asserted them to be provincial troops; fatally for we were not long deceived, the firing became every moment hotter; several cannon shot were fired without effect, and the grenadiers were ordered to the right about and march to the heights of which the rebels were already possessed; such a march may I never again experience.

We proceeded five miles in a road composed of nothing but sand which scorched through our shoes with intolerable heat; the sun beating on our heads with a force scarcely to be conceived in Europe, and not a drop of water to assuage our parching thirst; is it to be wondered that in these circumstances a number of the soldiers were unable to support the fatigue, and died on the spot. A corp. of the 43rd Grenadiers, who had by some means procured water, drank to such excess as to burst and expired in the utmost torments. Two became raving mad, and the whole road, strewed with miserable wretches wishing for death, exhibited the most shocking scene I ever saw.

At length we came within reach of the enemy who cannonaded us very briskly without doing much damage, am afterwards marching through a cornfield saw then drawn up behind a morass on a hill with a rail fence in front and a thick wood on their left filled with their light chosen troops. We rose on a small hill commanded by that on which they were posted in excellent order notwithstanding a heavy fire of grape, when judge of my inexpressible surprise, Gen. Clinton himself appeared at the head of our left wing accompanied by Lord Cornwallis, and crying out 'Charge, Grenadiers, never heed forming'; we rushed on amidst the heaviest fire I have yet felt.

It was no longer a contest for bringing up our respective companies in the best order, but all officers as well as soldiers strove who could be foremost, to my shame I speak it. I had the fortune to find myself after crossing the swamp with three officers only, in the midst of a large body of rebels who had been driven out of the wood by the 1st Battalion of Grenadiers, accompanied by not more than a dozen men who had been able to keep up with us; luckily the rebels were too intent on their own safety to regard our destruction. Lt. Bunbury of the [illeg.]

killed one of them with his sword, as we all might have done, but seeing a battalion running away with their colours, I pushed for them with the few fellows I had, but to my unutterable disappointment they out ran us in a second.

Col. Monckton was shot through the heart at the first charge, to the unspeakable loss of the regt. I have not now time to pay his virtues their just praise; his body which could not be found in the spot where he fell by a party I sent to bury it, was intered by the rebels the next day with military honours. Lt. Kennedy of the 44th Grenadiers, a relation of my Uncle Graham, was killed by the same fire. The column which we routed in this disorderly manner consisted of 4000, the force on our side not more than 800, during the whole our left flank was left flank entirely exposed and commanded by hills of which they afterwards availed themselves.

In the meantime the pursuit of this column brought us on their main army led by Washington, said by deserters to be 16000. With some difficulty we were brought in a disorderly manner under the hill we had gained, and the most terrible cannonade Ld. W. Erskine says he ever heard ensued and lasted for above two hours, at the distance of 600 yards; on our side two medium twelves, as many howitzers and 6 six-pounders which were answered by fourteen pieces, long twelves and french nines; our shells and twelves, which were admirably conducted by a Capt. Williams, did most horrible execution among their line drawn up on the hill. The shattered remains of our battalion, and part of the 1st who had joined us, being under cover of our hill suffered little, but from thirst and heat of which several died, except some who preferred the shade of some trees in the direct range of shot to the more horrid tortures of thirst.

Capt. Powell of the 52nd Grenadiers, one of these had his arm shattered to pieces; had my strength enabled me to have crawled so far I would most certainly preferred the chance of dying by a cannon ball. At length finding we did not take possession of the hills on their right, they brought some cannon on them and obliged us to move through the wood to a hill at a greater distance, and some brigades coming up both kept possession of their field from which they moved that evening, and we in the night. Our battalion lost 98, 11 officers killed and wounded, Major Gardner shot very badly through the foot.

I can only say that if you saw the situation in which I now write, all our things sent off and ourselves to move at daybreak; 10 o'clock at night when I was informed that the letters would be sent off tomorrow, the packet announced but yesterday, all our baggage gone You will excuse this incoherent letter and believe me your most affec. dutifull

W. Hale.

P.S. We are going to Long Island, the flank comp. to return to . . . ours and the 35th are apprised to be going to Halifax, our wounded left behind, among them Wills of Plym. who was in the 45th, his thigh shattered by a cannon ball, I am afraid you will scarcely be able to read this scrawl, with great difficulty from a corp. an extra half sheet to fold it in, even our adjutant has not a bit of paper left. Before the action began the Marquis La Fayette, who commanded the first part of the rebels we engaged, rode out and very politely saluted Major Gardner with whom he was formerly well acquainted in France.

I am told the general has expressed his approbation of the ridiculous behaviour of the four sub. officers I before mentioned who had got foremost, among these was my bro. officer who received a painful but not dangerous wound in the neck; the action happened at Freehold. All friends well. Courtenay and myself lay under the hill together during the cannonade, and swallowed a canteen of water which a tempting dollar from my pocket prevailed on an artillery driver to creep on all fours through the fire and fetch us at the imminent hazard of his life. God bless you, I will write more the first opportunity."

A letter written ten days later from New York announces that the 2nd Battalion of Grenadiers had been broken up, and the companies had returned to their respective regiments.

New York, 14th July, 1778.

The letter I had the pleasure of writing my dearest parents from the Neversunk was from the peculiar inconvenience of my situation almost illegible, yet I hope they will be able to perceive that I escaped unhurt in the very hot action of the 28th last month, allowed to be the severest that has happened, the rebel's cannon playing grape and case upon us at the distance of 40 yards and the small arms within little more than half that space; followed by a most incessant and terrible cannonade of near three hours' continuance; you may judge from the circumstance of our battalion guns, 6 pounders, firing 160 rounds, and then desisting only lest ammunition should be wanting for case shot; of the roar kept up by our twelves and howitzers, answered by near twenty pieces from their side on a hill 600 paces from ours.

The general's letter will inform you of the additional horrors of thirst, heat and fatigue which we had to encounter. I cannot sufficiently acknowledge the divine Goodness by which I was protected and preserved in good health amidst such accumulated dangers. On my arrival here I found my friend Williams very well and purser of the *Leviathan* store ship, where I am now writing, with the several packages under his care in good order. I before mentioned that I was in no immediate want of shirts, the other things were extremely acceptable, particularly the portable soup, some cakes of which I shall always keep in my pocket on a march. I should have been highly indebted to them on the day of engagement. Our comp. which I commanded lost 3 killed and one wounded, supposed mortally.

Our affairs wear at present a most desperate aspect; the Count D'Estaing with his fleet is now at anchor off the Hook, one 90, two 80's, nine 74's and 4 frigates. Lord How's small force of 6, 64, 4 fifties, two forties are drawn up in the form of a crescent in the channel, Admiral Byron is expected, or more properly hoped for with the greatest anxiety. The transports are all stript of their men, who voluntarily enlisted as soon as the French fleet was discovered; notwithstanding which the 15th and 44th together with the grenadiers and light companies of the 42nd and 17th are distributed among the men of war, some howitzers are carried to Paul's Hook, and a boom is preparing to be laid across the channel.

The general by his rashness in the last action has totally lost the confidence both of the officers and soldiers, who were astonished at seeing the commander of an army galloping like a Newmarket jockey at the head of a wing of grenadiers and expressly forbidding all form and order; the method too of dismissing the flank companies to their respective regiments gave no small disgust. After slightly thanking us for the ardour we had shewn, he repremanded us for disorder and plundering which never existed but among the followers of the army, and sent us about our business without even allotting boats to those whose regiments were not on the spot.

On more mature reflection however a letter was written to the officers commanding companies making some few compliments and assigning as a reason of our ungracious dismission, the probability of our being soon embodied again. I know not how affairs go on in England, but while I tremble for a revolution, I sincerely hope the punishment of those weak and wicked ministers who have prostituted the nation's honour in so shameful a manner. The loss of the gallant Colonel Monckton is one of the greatest misfortunes that could befall our regiment: no man was ever more sincerely and generally regretted. Major Gardner is yet in a very doubtful situation, the ball cannot be extracted, and the loss of his leg is extremely feared. Colonel Trelawney who was left with the rebels is here in a fair way of recovery; of the other wounded officers the reports are various and uncertain.

Wills is said by some to be dead, and by others doing well, the former is the most likely, the thigh being shattered too high for amputation. Our regiment is quartered comortably enough at Kingstown. Simcoe's wound is as slight as his former, not preventing him from doing his duty. I have been obliged to get the £20 I requested you from Williams, the arrival of our army having increased the price of everything to a most exorbitant rate. I paid yesterday for two yards and quarter of casimer and two pairs of waistcoats and trowsers of brown linen, without making, lining or trimmings, upwards of six guineas. I am persuaded you know me too well to imagine me capable of imposing on your goodness, but the greatest part of the army is ruined.

      W. Hale,

A week later he wrote again as follows:

      Camp at Kingsbridge, 21st July, 1778.
The present uncertainty of the packets reaching the place of destination induces me to miss no opportunity of acquainting my dearest parents of my perfect health, and preventing the apprehensions they would feel on the arrival of a packet without a letter from me at so critical a period as the present. Nothing has indeed happened since my last, worth notice; we

still remain blocked up, nor has any movement been made on either side; the French fleet continue in their former situation, and Lord How preserves his post at the Hook.

The *Leviathan*, formerly the *Northumberland* is nearly fitted out as a third-rate, and a further accession of strength is impatiently expected by the junction of the *Reasonable* and *Centurion*, both of whom are said to be in the Sound. Notwithstanding the truly alarming posture of affairs, New York is as busied as ever, nor does the least dejection or apprehension appear in the countenances of the merchants. Lord How, they say, is at the Hook, and their confidence in him is unbounded, he indeed fully deserves it; notwithstanding the nicety of his situation, and the difficulties with which he is surrounded, the same cool tranquillity and clearness attend all his orders, nor does he seem the least embarassed by the multiplicity of cares which must prey on his mind; his feelings must be exquisit but as they are confined to his own bosom, effect those under his command with no other passion than indignation at the shameful treatment experienced by the first officer in the British Navy.

The English are undeserving the services of a man who has any regard for his own honour, that of the nation is lost, and the ministers pay no regard to the feelings of individuals. Should they have sent Admiral Byron's fleet on any speculative plan, we are ruined, no object whatever could be equal to the preservation of this fleet and army, which will soon feel the want of the Cork Fleet; rice is already ordered to be issued twice a week instead of bread, and the daily decrease of provisions will unavoidably oblige Lord How, notwithstanding the inferiority of strength, to engage the French; he is now preparing for it, and when the three ships before mentioned have joined him an action may soon be expected. With regard to the situation of the army, reasons too obvious to mention forbid my entering on that branch of politics.

In my last I hinted at the disgust occasioned by the ungracious dismission of the flank corps, and that a letter was sent to the commanding officers of companies, on more mature reflection, pointing out the ill consequence of such a temper among the first and most serviceable part of the army. The following is a copy of that which I received, please to remark that it is dated many days prior to its circulation.

New York, 7th July, 1778.

Sir,

I am directed by Lord Rawdon to inform you and the other commanding officers of flank companies that your battalions are by no means to be considered from the order of yesterday as broken up, but are liable as soon as their accounts are settled, or upon the first prospect of movement, to be called together again, and for that reason your staff still subsists; that had not that been the case you may be assured the commander in chief has too just a sense of the very meritorious services of those corps to suffer them to pass unacknowledged. I am directed also to request that it may be explained to the men of those corps that it is merely the private economy of the army which has occasioned their being ordered to join their regiments for a time. I have the honour to be with respect.

Sir your most obd. Servant

G. Hutchinson, D. Adj. Gen.

This like all other palliations of undeserved injury was severely criticised, the words 'liable to be called together' was censured as implying our re-embodying to be the object of our dread rather than of our most sanguine wishes. Without descending to such niceties, I cannot help regarding it as a decent apology for an affront that was never meant, though it is said that the commanders of the first grenadiers and light infantry (Meadows and Abercromby) do not look on it as such. Whatever my opinion might have been, I have too much love for the grenadiers' line of service to quit it while able to go through its fatigues. I know not whether from want of inclination or abilities, but none of our generals have yet engaged more than three thousand of this army at one time, and in the last action scarce half that number was opposed to the whole rebel army; the brigades have been looked upon as nurseries only for the flank corps.

At Freehold indeed an attempt too late for success was made to employ them by General C. who seems to possess all the ideas, though it's feared not the abilities of a soldier. I mentioned to you that several of the flank companies were put on board the men of war, the whole are now said to be destined for that service. I should think the whole too many, however useful they might prove as veteran troops and on that account preferable to new raised marines, our distance will probably protect us, and the necessity of keeping a strong force at this place, and I have been so ill rewarded for my naval services, the taking and capture of a row galley at Philadelphia, which has never been publicly noticed, that I am determined to be content with [illeg.] that falls to my share on land unless ordered to the [illeg.]. . . .

> Your most dutifull etc
>
> W. Hale.

Lieutenant Hale took no part in any further operations in America. In a letter from Long Island, dated August 20, 1778, he says: "The report of our being drafted [gains] ground and is generally believed." As a matter of fact the report was correct, and the skeleton of the regiment, barely 100 strong, was sent home in the autumn.

In 1779 the county of Nottingham raised a considerable sum of money, and by means of a bounty of six guineas filled the 45th regiment up to strength. In consequence of this, the regiment was given the name of the Nottinghamshire Regiment—being the first regiment in the British Army to receive a county title.

In this letter young Hale refers as follows to the action between the *Isis* and the *Geli*, in which the light company of the 23rd took part as Marines:

The *Isis* too fell in with the *Geli*, their *Chef d'Escadre* of 74 guns, and after an engagement of two hours obliged her to bare away much shattered. The French commodore imagined from the silence on board the *Isis* that she meant to strike without resistance and bore down upon her within pistol shot, and gave three cheers which were answered by a broadside, and a smart action began, till some French rigging being shattered and the Isis to windward, Capt. Raynor availed himself of these circumstances and getting on his bow kept up a continued and well directed fire. Their musketry, of which they were full, was silenced by that of our marines and a detachment of the light comp. of the 23rd Reg. under the command of Capt. Smith.

At length by a variety of fortunate accidents the *Isis* got under her stern and gave her three broad-sides? on which she crowded all sail she could and got off, the *Isis* being too much damaged to obstruct or pursue her. A corpl. only of the 23rd was killed, and very few wounded, numbers of the French were seen thrown overboard during the action; during which a very genteel man was observed to come from the cabin of the *Geli* to the stern gallery and throw some papers overboard after tearing them; on his return to the deck the light infantry singled him out and shot him dead, it is thought he was the commodore. On the *Geli* bearing away, the light infantry, who fixed their bayonets and wanted to board gave the Indian war hoop.

In a letter from Exeter, dated December 2, young Hale announces his safe arrival at home, and then adds:

Of public affairs the packet which sailed after us has brought news and more ample accounts than I can give, you will there see how Gen. Clinton surprised 150 horse, how he went into the Jersies for hay, how he did not bring back half sufficient, and how he is at a loss where to go for more, having very kindly suffered the farmers on the different islands to dispose of their forage to whom and in what quantities they pleased, without reserving any for the magazine. Gen. Grant, remarkable for his activity, diligence and success . . . at table . . . is gone with ten regiments to the West Indies on whom the Lord have mercy.
A letter I saw yesterday says it is thought they are going against St. Lucia by way of reprisal for Dominica; if so we shall probably hear of a miscarriage very soon. An expedition to the south-ward also talked of and the regiments appointed, but the commander not fixed upon; indeed I should apprehend they would be not a little puzzled to find one capable of commanding two or three thousand men.
You will easily believe my wardrobe is not the best furnished after so long absence; so that I must beg the favour of you to send the inclosed measures to Ireland the taylor for a suit of full regimentals, the embroidery he will see at Plumers, lined with silk, two epaulets which must not be sewed on, and the facings a deep green. To say the truth I have but one coat and an old campaign jacket. I mention this scanty apparatus as an inducement to hasten Mr. Ireland's operations, lest I should be altogether confined before its arrival. Such was the excessive price of cloth at New York that I thought it needless to provide cloths for Europe.

Young Hale was promoted captain into the 94th Foot on March 3,

1780, and retired on December 5 of the following year. He married in 1783, and lived at Chudleigh in Devonshire till his death in 1789.

WILLIAM JOHN HALE.

Lieutenant, 45th Foot, March 2, 1776.

Captain, 94th Foot, March 3, 1780 (retired December 5, 1781).

www.ingramcontent.com/pod-product-compliance
Lightning Source LLC
Chambersburg PA
CBHW021056090426
42738CB00006B/364